CW00428114

GRILL STOCK ®

THE

BBQ

BOOK

MEAT.MUSIC.MAYHEM

DEDICATION

For Marie-Louise, Matilda,
Noah & Jake – JF

For my rockin'
wife Esme – BM

GRILL STOCK ®

★ ★ ★ ★ ★ ★ ★ ★ ★ ★ ★ ★ ★ ★ ★

— THE —

BBQ

BOOK

★ ★ ★ ★ ★ ★ ★ ★ ★ ★ ★ ★ ★ ★ ★

MEAT.MUSIC.MAYHEM

★ ★ ★ ★ ★ ★ ★ ★ ★ ★ ★ ★ ★ ★ ★

★ ★ ★ JON FINCH & BEN MERRINGTON ★ ★ ★

CONTENTS

FOREWORD BY
RAY LAMPE, DR. BBQ

In early 2010 I sent a very random email through the Grillstock website. I was enquiring on behalf of the grill company I work for. I was hoping that this new festival in the UK would welcome a veteran American BBQ man and possibly trade a sponsorship for my participation. I had no idea who would read the email and whether they knew who I was, or cared. Jon Finch replied and said they were very interested. That moment changed both of our lives for ever.

Jon worked it out with the grill company and I attended the first ever Grillstock Festival in Bristol. It was clearly a new event run by a new team, but there were dynamic people in the mix and it was clear that Jon and his business partner, Ben Merrington, had a vision. Their vision was a fun festival for all that included great music, great BBQ, and a host of fun characters all built around an American-style BBQ competition. Their one problem was that they hadn't ever been behind the scenes at an American BBQ competition and weren't quite sure how best to run one. Frankly, neither was anyone else in the UK at that time. That's where I came in.

I began my career as a BBQ competitor in 1982 – the same year Ben was born! Back then it was my hobby and I was successful, winning more than 300 awards. In 2000 my personal life took a wicked turn, so I closed the family trucking business in Chicago and moved to Florida to pursue BBQ as my business. Since then I have done just about everything there is to do in the BBQ world: some good and some bad, but all a great learning experience. I was the BBQ expert who could give Grillstock credibility, but I could also provide guidance. For me it was another great adventure and a chance to share the BBQ knowledge that I love so much with the rest of the world. A perfect pairing.

Over the years, Jon, Ben and I have established a great working relationship. Jon and Ben have become serious festival organizers and strong restaurateurs, and they've certainly learned a thing or two about how to cook BBQ. But they are never above referring any old-school questions to me. We've become great friends, too. In 2014 I was inducted into the BBQ Hall Of Fame and standing next to my fiancée, Sandi, in Kansas City, watching as I was inducted, were Jon Finch and Ben Merrington. I will never forget their pleasure in being there, and mine in having them. These are great young entrepreneurs with good minds for business and the aforementioned vision of what Grillstock should be. That vision combined with Ben's unique eye for style and design has matured over the six years and at a recent festival the guests saw a pretty good version of what Grillstock is meant to be.

But there is no complacency. These guys are young and their creativity and energy will continue to evolve Grillstock for a long time to come. I, for one, can't wait to see what's next. Congratulations guys on the book. It's beautiful and I'm happy to see you share the things you've learned together along the way. I wish you all the best with it and I'm all in for the next chapter of Grillstock.

Ray Lampe, Dr. BBQ

ABOUT GRILLSTOCK

Sitting by the smoker back in 2009, we dreamt up the idea of bringing competition BBQ to the UK. The plan was simple: to create something that would gather mates and strangers together to drink, eat, laugh, and basically have some fun. Nothing fancy or complicated. We were just two ordinary blokes with the simple need to have a good time and smoke some meat – and not much has changed. We wanted to give other people a place to enjoy the good stuff that always makes us happy – good company, good food, good drink and good music...

That's Grillstock.

Nothing's really ever simple, though – organizing big festivals and BBQ competitions, opening Smokehouses, even choosing the right ingredients for our house sauce – everything takes time and patience, trial and error, and a lot of late nights over many beers to really get right. We had our first festival in 2010 and opened our first Smokehouse two years later, and we're still learning, refining, inventing.

When we stand at the back of the main stage at one of our festivals and watch thousands of people wave their arms in the air in time to the music, it makes all the hard work worthwhile. It's the same when we see one of our restaurants packed out and buzzing. We don't feel that way because we think we've achieved something no one else could achieve. It's just because we are genuinely stoked that we give those people something to wave their arms about. They're with us, loving the stuff that we love. Meat, music, mayhem for all.

Along the way, Grillstock has enabled us to meet some remarkable people as well as learn about how to cook, serve and live BBQ. It's given us the chance to have the best job in the world. This book is our opportunity to share our favourite bits of Grillstock with you. If you're cooking BBQ with this book open beside you, pages all sticky with sauce and a bit charred at the edges, having a few beers with your mates, sitting by your fire and having fun, then our work is done.

Jon and Ben

COMPETITION BBQ – GETTING INTO THE PIT

Competition BBQ needs to be your new favourite hobby. It's a legitimate excuse to hang out with your mates, playing with fire, cooking meat, and drinking beer and bourbon for 48 hours – even at the practice sessions at home. And if you compete at Grillstock, you get to listen to some awesome live music and show off your skills to thousands of people, too. First and foremost, competing is damn good fun – but there is a serious side.

There's big prize money at stake. For teams that are consistently winning, competition is often a route to bigger adventures: travelling the world like rock stars, opening a restaurant or catering business, launching a BBQ sauce, and often much more.

Like many things, the keys to winning are attention to detail and putting in the practice. Perfection is in the weeks, months and years teams spend evolving their own rubs and sauces; the countless hours refining cooking techniques, fettling equipment, mixing smoking woods and practising competition cooks at home. It's a never-ending cycle of always making better, always looking for the edge.

More attention is paid to a piece of meat in competition BBQ than in any kitchen anywhere in the world. Pitmasters will sit up all night babysitting their brisket, rubbing, basting, spritzing, wrapping, probing, doing everything to ensure their eight perfect slices presented at the judges' table the following day are better than everyone else's.

Competition BBQ is the best BBQ you can eat.

That's why we've asked some of the teams (and rock stars) whose lifeblood is pure competition BBQ to contribute to our book. Their wisdom is BBQ gold.

Walking through the bustling competition pits early in the morning before festival visitors arrive is utopia for us. The smells, the sounds, the flavours are unlike anything you can find elsewhere. These moments are the constant source of inspiration for our Smokehouses and our own flavours.

Bringing true competition BBQ to the UK is why we started back in 2010 and it remains just as important to us today. The heart and soul of the Grillstock Festivals is 'King of the Grill', a huge two-day, US-style, low-'n'-slow BBQ competition with dozens of teams battling it out over the smoky coals to be crowned Grand Champion.

Grand Champions win all kinds of cool stuff, including a wedge of cash, a custom cigar-box guitar, a massive trophy, and entry to other worldwide BBQ competitions. But, above all, they win ultimate bragging rights. Respect.

Over the Saturday and Sunday of the festival, teams work tirelessly – often sleeplessly – to 'turn in' seven meaty categories to a panel of between five and seven judges. The judges are drawn from BBQ experts, chefs, true foodies... and, of course, our own pit-lovin' selves. These King of the Grill aficionados take bite after juicy bite from the food turned in by our amazing teams. As they taste, the judges allocate a point score (out of 100 altogether) for every dish. There are guidelines for how to give the points, of course – we've put them in a handy box on page 14, in case you ever want to be a BBQ judge yourself (we recommend it – it's awesome).

The seven competition categories we give our bold and brave pitmasters are the same as the chapters of our book. (Well, almost – there's a competition category for Wings, too, but we've put wings in our Chicken chapter, to keep things simple.) Here's what every competition team produces:

PORK

We see Boston butt, picnic and/or whole shoulder, and have it cooked as a single piece of meat. Judges look for the meat to have been teased apart, not overworked, combined with a good chew and flavour from the bark (the crust on the outside of the meat). The rub will be prominent, and balanced with the rest of the flavours. Sauce in competition BBQ usually errs heavily on sweet and heat, with a good vinegary kick in the back.

RIBS

For competition, we accept pork spare ribs, or loin or baby back ribs only. Judges look for seven or eight identical-looking, neatly trimmed ribs, each with a flawless saucy glaze. Spare ribs are usually the pitmasters' choice, as they offer more flavour and chew. They are also slightly more forgiving to cook, being that they are larger and fattier than their smaller baby back cousins. Ribs should pack a big punch of rub, smoke and sauce flavours – all in perfect harmony and none overpowering the rib meat itself. A team will instantly lose points for any signs that rib membrane (see box, p.52) has been left in place before cooking. That's just laziness.

BRISKET

A cut of beef taken from the chest of the cow, brisket is made up of two parts – the flat (the widest, meatiest part) and the point (the narrower, fattier end). An entry to the judges' table might be the whole brisket, or one or other part – but usually it combines a number of identical-looking slices from the leaner flat, as well as some juicy, sticky burnt ends on the side. These are made from the fattier point section. Smoke rings (literally, a pinker ring around the edge of each brisket slice) will gain valuable points. The meat should be juicy and... well, beefy... and served without a sauce. Serving up dry brisket is BBQ suicide.

CHICKEN

Chicken may be cooked whole, halved or in pieces. Typically, pitmasters will turn in smoked chicken thighs (see p.98), which are less prone to drying out during smoking, and carry more flavour than the breast. We see real skill when the skin is 'bite-through' and the meat is succulent and delicious.

CHEF'S CHOICE

The dishes in this category can be anything the team wishes to enter, providing the main component is cooked on a BBQ. Pitmasters can really show some creativity, flair and panache. We've seen some eye-popping entries over the years – from a three-tier, pork-pie wedding cake and a roast chicken riding a metal motorbike to a metre-tall tower of moink balls, as well as eel sushi, gumbo, a whole roast lamb, and a whole suckling pig.

BURGERS

A competition burger is a patty of ground beef or alternative – and it's what's between the bun or bread we're judging. Some teams go for toppings that are crazy, exotic and awe-inspiring. Others go simple. Experience tells us that while a creative-looking burger may score points for appearance, the winners are usually the guys that make a simple burger – but do it very, very well.

WINGS

Teams turn in part or whole chicken wings, and this round is about fun... and heat. Maybe we should rename it the 'Scoville Round' – after the Scoville Scale that measures chilli strength. Some of those wings are so hot we make Wings' judges sign a disclaimer before they bite. Glass of milk, anyone?

HOW TO BE A COMPETITION JUDGE

When your best BBQ buddy sidles up to you with some smoky goodness he's been perfecting for months, this is how you give him your official judge's opinion of his efforts. (You're scoring out of 100, remember.)

1. Appearance (max. 20 points): How appetizing does the dish look? You're taking the first bite with your eyes to get those taste buds going.

2. Texture (max. 30 points): Is the meat moist and easy to chew? Does it pull easily from the bone, but retain body, with moisture and texture?

3. Taste (max. 50 points): Are there smoke and flavours cooked into the meat? What magic is the rub working? Does the sauce add to the goodness, or (BBQ sinners beware) clash with it?

GRILL STOCK®

JUDGING SLIP

CATEGORY PLEASE TICK

CHICKEN ☐   RIBS ☐   PORK ☐   BRISKET ☒

LAMB ☐   DESSERT ☐   CHEF'S CHOICE ☐

SCORE

APPEARANCE OF ENTRY - AWARD 0-20 POINTS

TEXTURE OF ENTRY - AWARD 0-30 POINTS

TASTE OF ENTRY - AWARD 0-50 POINTS

TEAM NO.	TASTE	TEXTURE	APPEARANCE
14	35	23	18
15	42	30	15
16	33	27	19
17	45	21	10
18			
19			

BBQ LIKE A BAD-ASS

GET WELL-OILED BEFORE YOU BEGIN

Before and after every session, you should clean and oil your grill. Get it nice and hot to burn off any crud, then, using tongs, rub it all over with a kitchen towel dipped in a light cooking oil. When you've finished cooking for the day, open up all the vents and burn the grill clean again. This keeps your grill hygienic, as well as helping prevent food from sticking to the bars.

KNOW YOUR RIG

Everybody's BBQ cooks differently – get to know yours and how it cooks, and you'll soon learn how to quickly set it up for different types of cooking and how to manage its fire and heat. The BBQ temperatures we've given in the book are very much a rough guide; and readings from the temperature gauge in your BBQ are best treated as merely a suggestion of the actual heat. We recommend hovering your hand over the coals to gauge temperature. The sooner your hand hurts, the hotter the coals. With a bit of trial and error, you'll soon learn the optimum heat for grilling, for roasting, and for smoking on your own rig.

You'll also need to learn the best way to keep a consistent cooking temperature, especially with the longer slow cooks. A chimney starter is a crucial piece of kit for this – it allows you to add lit coals to the fire, replenishing it when you need to.

KNOW YOUR PIG

Always start with great meat – and not just pork. It stands to reason that the better the quality of meat you start off with, the better the end result.

SET UP YOUR GRILL

Always use natural lumpwood charcoal – the bigger the chunks, the better. It's far easier to light, burns cleaner and more consistently, gives off a better flavour and leaves far less ash than briquettes. NEVER EVER use 'instant light' charcoal laced with lighter fuel or the BBQ Mafia will hunt you down.

ALL THE GEAR...

You don't need tons of fancy kit to cook and smoke meat. Mankind has been slow-cooking meat for thousands of years and our ancestors never had a shedful of gadgets. There are, though, some bits and pieces that modern times have given us that will make your cookout much easier and make sure your meat comes out the best it can. They are:

- a chimney starter – for easy lighting and also replenishing of coals

- an instant-read thermometer – for perfect doneness

- thick heatproof gloves – for moving hot stuff around without burning yourself

- a very sharp knife

- a basting brush for glazing and saucing

- good-quality, heatproof tongs (we like the OXO brand)

- thick tin foil – the thickest you can buy, like the catering stuff. Costco own brand is good

There are four primary ways to cook on a BBQ – directly, two-zone, indirectly, and smoking.

DIRECT COOKING
Spread your lit coals out in a single, even layer. Apart from steaks and burgers, very little calls for a screaming-hot direct grill. Far better is to use slightly fewer coals and allow them to burn down to a consistent medium grilling heat. There will be fewer flare-ups and less chance of incinerating your food.

TWO-ZONE COOKING

Our 'go-to' technique for setting up a BBQ is to have two cooking zones. You cook pretty much everything this way. Set up so you have one zone directly over the coals for searing, and another cooler zone, away from the coals, to allow the meat to cook through indirectly. With a charcoal grill just pile up your coals on one side, leaving the other side clear. Use more coal and open the vents to increase the airflow to cook at higher temperatures. Clamp the airflow down and close the lid (if your BBQ has one) to reduce the temperature for a slow, controlled, indirect burn.

INDIRECT COOKING

To cook indirectly set up your BBQ for two-zone cooking, as above, then use only the cooler side of the grill, away from the hot coals. If you have a lid, keep it closed as much as possible during cooking. This way the heat circulates to cook the food evenly.

SMOKING

Smoking is the ultimate in low 'n' slow. It is always indirect cooking at a low temperature. Ideally, you'll do this in a dedicated smoker built for the purpose, which will be able to smoke for a long time without the need for replenishing the coals too often. In the absence of a purpose-built smoker, you can smoke in pretty much any BBQ with a lid.

Smoking on a kettle BBQ

Most of us begin BBQing using a kettle BBQ. That's a good thing as kettles are widely available, reasonably priced and incredibly versatile. The Weber kettle BBQ is tried-and-tested and has been around for decades. You can grill, roast and smoke anything on a kettle. To set up your kettle to smoke (see our handy diagram, right, too):

1. Add lit coals from a chimney starter to one side of the grate (as for two-zone cooking, above).

2. Place a foil tray on the other side of the grate and part fill it with hot water – this will help to regulate the cooking temperature as well as act as a drip pan.

3. Add wood chunks (see p.22) to the hot coals and replace the grill rack.

4. Place the meat on the grill rack over the foil tray.

5. Keep an eye on the temperature gauge and add more lit coals if you need to.

Smoking on a gas BBQ

Well, yes, technically you can. But we'd prefer it if you didn't – you'll miss out on half the fun and half the flavour.

PLAY WITH SMOKE

Smoke is a seasoning, so learn to add subtle smoke flavour to your food. Everything in balance, though – you want to be able to taste the rub, the sauce, the meat and the smoke all in heavenly harmony. You'll get a background smoke flavour from using decent, natural lumpwood charcoal. Then, use wood chunks to add that extra-special layer on top.

Wood chunks between the size of a golf and tennis ball are best. Don't bother soaking them first, just throw them straight onto the coals just before you add the meat, and they'll smoulder away for ages. Wood chips tend to burn up too quickly directly on coals, but if you have a gas BBQ, wrapping some up in a couple of layers of thick foil and piercing it a few times, before throwing the parcel onto the grill over the burners works well. Check out our guide to wood-smoke flavours on page 22.

LEARN TO GIVE A DAMN GOOD RUB

BBQ is about building up layers of flavour so the resulting mouthfuls of meat knock your socks off. A BBQ rub is probably the most important part of this – it's where the main flavour profile comes from. It's the foundation for the whole recipe that ties the flavours of the meat, the sauce and the wood smoke together. It's also the base of the wonderful dark bark that builds up on the meat during cooking. That's the heavily seasoned, smoky, chewy exterior that everyone wants part of in their sandwich.

Develop your own base or house rub (see p.201), then use this as a starting point to develop other rubs according to the flavours you enjoy. Rubs should be balanced and offer some heat, some sweet and a good, rounded background seasoning.

Apply your rub to the surface of the meat, then pat it down or massage it in. Don't aim for a thick coating like bread-crumbing – a rub forms a thin, uniform, consistent and even layer (see photographs, opposite).

Generally, the larger the cut of meat, the further ahead you can rub. So, you can rub your ribs up to about six hours in advance (any more and the meat starts to cure and you'll get a weird ham-like flavour). Pork shoulders or briskets on the other hand can cope with a good overnight rest bathed in rub.

SLOW THINGS DOWN, RELAX...

True BBQ takes time and patience. The meat is done when it's done – don't try to rush things. Accept that this is a slow process and allow yourself to enjoy it. Find yourself a comfy chair and position it near your smoker. Fill a bucket with ice and some beers, turn on some tunes and spend the afternoon keeping your meat company as it goes on its smoky journey of love. If anyone tries to give you chores to do, sorry, you can't help. You're busy cooking.

DON'T FIDDLE AND POKE

And definitely don't squeeze. Once you've put the meat on the grill just leave it. You should turn the meat only once or twice throughout grilling. Squashing burgers and steaks down on the grill just squeezes out all the lovely juice and causes flare-ups. Tut-tut.

CHECK FOR DONENESS

Overcooking is as sinful as undercooking. Invest in a good instant-read thermometer so you know the exact temperature of your meat – it takes away the guesswork. Thermometer in hand, you'll always know the chicken is cooked through and you'll be able to serve up the perfect medium–rare steak.

It's impossible to give accurate cooking times for true low 'n' slow BBQ. There are so many variables in play – the heat of your fire, the ambient air temp, the size and fat content of the joint of meat, the distance of the meat from the coals you're cooking on, and so on. It's also impossible to give specific cooking temperatures – your BBQ cooks differently

GRILLING TEMPERATURES

If your BBQ has a temperature gauge, these are the rough target temps to aim for:

- Low 'n' slow/smoking: around 110–120°C
- Medium: around 150–180°C
- High: around 200–250°C

from your neighbour's and many BBQs don't have an accurate temperature gauge (or one at all). The little guide in the box above will give you an indication of what we mean by low, medium and high grill heat, but it is by no means foolproof. In good time, you'll get to know the way your BBQ cooks.

Instead, aiming for specific internal temperatures (we give these in each of the recipes) will make sure your pork pulls properly and your ribs have that perfect bite to them. Follow the basic rules of how to set up your cooker for the different styles and then let the meat tell you when it is done.

DON'T GET SAUCY UNTIL THE END

BBQ sauces and glazes have a high sugar content that will burn very quickly and go bitter if left cooking for too long. Cook your meat through, then glaze or sauce towards the end of cooking and allow the meat to go sticky over a gentler, indirect heat.

BE A MEAT WHISPERER

True BBQ is not about exact recipes, timings or precise cooking temperatures. Anyone can mix up a rub or buy a bottle of sauce, and – more importantly – we're cooking with live fire here, it's not like switching on your oven. Understand your rig and the basic cooking techniques and then watch, feel, smell, taste and listen carefully to your meat. It tells you what adjustments it needs and when it's done.

DON'T COOK IN FLIP-FLOPS

Trust us on that – we've learned it the hard way many times over.

SMOKING WOODS

There are two main types of smoking wood – hardwoods and fruit woods. It's nice to mix them up and come up with a custom blend of your own. In the Smokehouses we smoke with a mixture of oak and hickory wood. The oak provides a consistent heat and a solid, well-rounded background smoke flavour. The hickory gives a punchy, nutty smokiness that works well. Too much hickory would be a little overpowering. Never use softwoods – they are too resinous and give off bitter flavours. Here's our Grillstock guide to wood flavour:

ALDER
Delicate and subtle with a slight sweetness, alder is easily lost in the background, particularly when you use big-hitting rubs and sauces.

APPLE
Applewood is lovely and widely available. Less powerful than oak, it is a good all-rounder that you can use to smoke anything and has a sweetness that comes through in the final meat.

BEECH
A moderate all-rounder, beech works well with all meats.

CHERRY
Similar to applewood, but a little more aromatic and rich, cherry is another great all-rounder. It gives a slight pinkish colour to light meats. Many people choose cherry as their favourite.

HICKORY
The daddy of smoking woods, hickory has a similar flavour to oak, but with a little more kick and a sweet, nutty aroma. Chips are widely available in the UK, but chunks not so much.

MESQUITE
This wood has long been associated with smoking, but our advice is to steer clear. Mesquite is overpowering and pungent, and it can be bitter.

OAK
An awesome all-rounder and very widely available, oak gives a punchy smoke flavour and is good to use as a base to mix in with other smoking woods.

PEAR
Almost identical in texture and flavour to applewood, pear is great if you can get hold of it.

PECAN
This smoking wood is our personal favourite, but it's hard to get in the UK. Pecan gives a wonderful, balanced sweet, rounded, nutty flavour. If you ever see some pecan chunks, buy them.

WALNUT
With its big, heavy and punchy smoke flavour, walnut will overpower lighter meats, such as chicken and pork. But, it works well if you're looking for a big smoke hit on briskets.

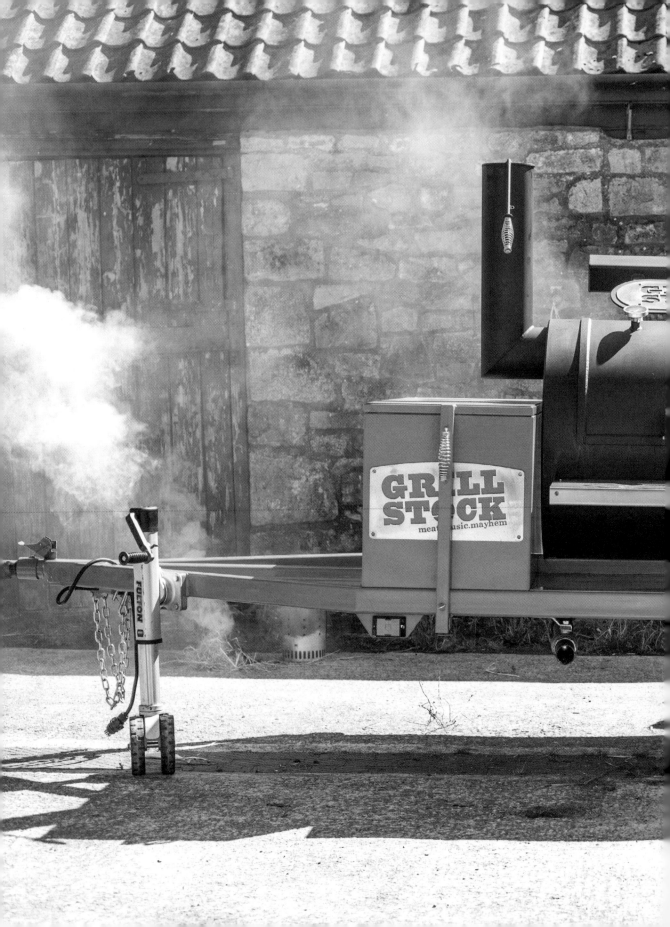

PORK

SMOKEHOUSE PULLED PORK

The cornerstone of pit-BBQ and a 'must-master' dish for any pitmaster, pork shoulder is top of the list for being the biggest, toughest, fattiest slab of meat there is. But, its transformation when treated to 18 hours of wood smoke is as beautiful as you will find anywhere in nature: smoky, dark, chewy, seasoned bark opens to reveal steaming hunks of succulent and juicy pork just waiting to be teased apart.

Buy pork shoulder from your butcher – smaller cuts in supermarkets don't cook up properly. We order ours at around 6 to 8kg – a big hunk of meat that can spend a long time in the smoke.

FEEDS ABOUT 20

INGREDIENTS

6–8kg bone-in pork shoulder, skin removed and fat trimmed to 5mm thick

Grillstock House Rub (see p.202)

250ml Backyard BBQ Sauce (see p.194)

250ml apple juice

The rest

Tom Herbert's Buns (see p.168), split and lightly toasted

Damn Fast Awesome Pickles (see p.178)

House Slaw (see p.184)

METHOD

1. An hour or so before you plan to start cooking, liberally season the pork all over with the rub. Leave the pork to come to room temperature.

2. Set up your BBQ for smoking (see p.19), around 110°C. Add your choice of smoking wood to the coals – we like to use pecan, hickory or fruit wood with pork.

3. Put the pork on the BBQ, fat-side up, and smoke for around 8 hours, or until the outside of the pork has a wonderful dark bark and the meat can easily be pulled away from the bone. The internal temperature should hit 92°C.

4. Transfer the pork to a large tray, cover tightly with foil and leave to rest for 30 minutes.

5. Pull the meat away from the bone in hunks and then tease the strands apart with a meat shredder or your fingers, making sure the deliciously seasoned bark is distributed evenly throughout so everyone gets a taste.

6. Mix together the BBQ sauce and apple juice. Pour the mixture over the pork and gently turn until coated, taking care not to break it up any further. Serve the pork in buns with pickles and slaw.

Alternatively, sprinkle the pork with a little more rub and serve it with the BBQ sauce on the side.

PITMASTER'S BREAKFAST

Smoking a big ol' pork shoulder usually means getting up early to check your hunk of loveliness had a good night's sleep in the smoke, monitor the internal temp and make sure the coals are still smouldering. If you've mastered the management of the fire for long cooks, your pork should be sitting at a perfect 92°C for you, waiting to be wrapped and rested until your guests arrive for lunch. Your reward for all this hard work is a Pitmaster's Breakfast (we have one every Friday and Saturday morning at our St Nick's shack in Bristol). It's what a McMuffin® dreams of becoming.

FEEDS 1

INGREDIENTS

chunk of Smokehouse Pulled Pork (see p.29), fresh off the smoker, or leftovers are good

small knob of butter or a splash of oil, plus extra for frying egg

a splash of apple juice

1 American-style cheese slice

1 egg

The rest

1 Tom Herbert's Bun (see p.168), split and lightly toasted

a splash of Frank's RedHot sauce (optional)

METHOD

① Using a pair of tongs, tug off a hunk of the pork shoulder. Choose a bit with the nicest looking bark — it's your treat. Leave the rest of the shoulder on the smoker while you have your much-deserved breakfast.

② Back in the kitchen, heat the butter or oil in a frying pan over a medium heat.

③ Shred the pork and place it in the frying pan in a small pile. Cook for a few minutes until the bottom of the pork starts to caramelize, drizzle over a little apple juice and place the cheese on top. Cover with a lid for 30 seconds or until heated through.

④ Remove the porky pile from the pan and cover loosely with foil to keep it warm while you cook the egg. Use the same pan to fry the egg, adding more butter or oil if you need to.

⑤ Fill the bun with the pork and cheese. Top with the fried egg and a splash of Frank's RedHot sauce, if you like. Enjoy with a mug of coffee.

VENTURE INTO THE DAY KNOWING YOU'VE EATEN A BETTER BREAKFAST THAN ANYONE ELSE: A BREAKFAST OF CHAMPIONS.

CHERRY-SMOKED PORK BELLY

Pork belly is where streaky bacon comes from, but in this dish we're going to slow smoke it whole, so that much of the fat renders out and keeps the meat juicy and tasty. It works with a kick of sweetness, so we're hitting it up with a mixture of regular house rub and then some sweet rub. It's kind of like a candied-bacon, sweet-and-salty thing. Mmm... bacon...

Use a smaller piece of pork belly if you're cooking for fewer people, but keep the cooking time more-or-less the same. How long you cook is dictated more by the thickness of the slab you buy than by the square footage.

We'd suggest removing the skin (it goes tough and gnarly in a smoker), but don't throw it away – you can make crackling with it separately.

FEEDS 12–15

INGREDIENTS

Grillstock House Rub (see p.202)

Sweet Rub (see p.206)

5kg pork belly, skin removed, leaving a 1cm layer of fat

Hot BBQ Sauce (see p.194) or North Carolina Sauce (see p.197), to serve

METHOD

① Mix together the house rub and sweet rub in equal proportion.

② Liberally season the pork belly all over with the rub mix. Leave it to stand for an hour or two while the rub works its sweet and salty magic and the pork comes up to room temperature.

③ Set up your BBQ for smoking (see p.19), around 110°C. Add your choice of smoking wood to the coals – we like to use cherry or other fruit woods.

④ Put the pork on the BBQ, fat-side up, and smoke for 6–7 hours or until the outside of the belly has developed a lovely dark bark, similar to that of slow-cooked pork shoulder (see p.29). The fat should be loose and wet with the meat still retaining a good bite. The internal temperature should hit around 80°C.

⑤ Transfer the pork to a large tray, cover tightly with foil and leave to rest for 20 minutes.

⑥ You can serve the pork in any number of ways: pulled in pretty much the same way as a pork shoulder (see p.29); in a roll; sliced and served with fixin's on the side; or just put the whole belly on a board with BBQ sauce and let everyone tuck in.

JEDI SWINE TRICKS' STEPHEN HEYES IS ONE OF THE MOST
EXPERIENCED AND DECORATED COMPETITION BBQ COOKS IN
THE UK, AND A LEGEND AMONG HIS PEERS – BOTH FOR FEEDING
THE CROWDS AND FOR PARTYING LIKE A BANSHEE.

JEDI SWINE TRICKS'
★ COMPETITION PORK ★

FEEDS 6–10

INGREDIENTS

3–5kg Boston butt (pork shoulder on the bone)

demerara sugar

sea salt

SAUCE

250ml ketchup

125ml apple juice

2 tbsp apple cider vinegar

¼ tsp onion powder

¼ tsp garlic powder

¼ tsp chilli flakes

2 tsp mustard powder

2 tbsp light soft brown sugar

2 tbsp molasses

⅛ tsp liquid smoke

2 tbsp lemon juice

2 tbsp honey

1 tsp coarsely ground black pepper

sea salt, to taste

INJECTION

200ml pineapple juice

200ml apple juice

2 tbsp red wine vinegar

2 tbsp honey

1 tbsp sriracha sauce

½ tsp sea salt

1 chicken stock cube

FOIL MARINADE

200ml apple juice

100ml water

2 tbsp red wine vinegar

100g light soft brown sugar

2 tbsp olive oil

2 tbsp Worcestershire sauce

1 tbsp BBQ sauce

1 tsp rub (as below)

½ tsp cayenne pepper

RUB

2 tbsp golden caster sugar

1 tbsp demerara sugar

1 tbsp + 1 tsp garlic salt

1 tbsp + 1 tsp onion salt

2 tsp celery salt

1 tsp sea salt

2 tbsp paprika

1 tbsp freshly ground black pepper

2 tsp ancho chilli powder

½ tsp chipotle powder

¼ tsp ground cumin

METHOD

First, get your rubs and sauces together. Really you want to do your BBQ sauce a few days in advance so it has time to mature.

Making the sauce is simple: put all your ingredients minus salt and pepper in a big non-reactive pan, bring to the boil, then simmer for 20 minutes. Taste it and season with salt until you're happy. I find a couple of pinches does it. Add the black pepper and simmer for 10 minutes more. Transfer to a suitable container and stick it in the fridge where it will happily sit for 6 weeks.

Injection - simple again (you see a recurring theme here): mix all the ingredients in a pan, bring to the boil, simmer until your stock cube has dissolved, then remove from the heat and chill down. This is best done 1 or 2 days before you cook your butt.

Foil marinade and rub - yep it's getting more simple. To make each of these, you just put the relevant ingredients together, mix well and that's it. I recommend making these one day in advance to let the flavours combine.

NOW WE GET TO THE PROPER PART AND THE FIRST THING YOU DO IS TRIM UP THAT BUTT.

If it has a fat cap and rind on it, whip it off using a boning knife. There's a misconception that the fat cap keeps the meat moist, but it's the fat and collagen tuning through the butt that does this. The fat cap just reduces the surface area available for rub, so reducing the amount of lovely bark you can achieve.

Remove any loose, dangly or blood-stained fat, and any vein ends, too. For competition-style butts, partially separate the money muscle - just loosen it slightly so you can get a little more rub around it. The money muscle is the absolute best bit of the butt - so take your time.

Once the butt's trimmed, inject it evenly all over with your injection. Don't overfill or the marinade will just leak out. I find 3-4ml per hole works well.

Now it's time to rub. There's an optional comp trick here. A light dusting of sea salt before you rub gives more punch - you want this for the judges as they get only one bite. If you're at home, though, you can omit this step.

Now, rub time. Put a nice, even coating of rub all over. Pat it in rather than actually rubbing, then wrap the butt tightly in cling film. Leave this bad boy in the fridge for at least 4 hours.

Set up your smoker to run at 110°C for 9 hours (you'll ramp it up to 130°C for another 3-4 hours after this).

Half an hour before you get your butt on the smoker, grab it out of the fridge, unwrap and lightly dust it with demerara sugar. The extra sugar will accelerate the Maillard effect, giving you improved bark.

NOW, JUST SLAM YOUR BUTT IN THE SMOKER, SHUT THAT LID AND DON'T OPEN IT FOR 9 HOURS.

I typically add my wood at this point: fist-sized chunks of hickory and cherry nestled into the burning coals.

Keep an eye on the temps. Stick around the 110°C mark. Remember, though, when you first chuck in a large piece of meat, you'll get a drop, so leave it 20 minutes before you play with your vents. If your temperature overshoots, don't open the pit to try to burp it. This doesn't work – the BBQ pixies know you've been naughty, so they come and stoke your fire. Actually, that's a lie. In reality, the pit burps, and the fire gets a gulp of oxygen and burns harder. To take the heat out, just spray the lid with water using a household plant sprayer.

After 9 hours, lift that lid and check out your lovely pork. It'll look good enough to eat, but don't be tempted... patience Padawan! Take the butt from the smoker and wrap it tightly in a double layer of foil with half of the foil marinade. Seal it completely.

Return the pork to the smoker, start ramping to 130°C and cook for another 3-4 hours. You want an internal temperature of around 93°C, but the way it feels when you probe it is more important. When the pork is done, probing feels like pushing a knife into hot butter: soft with little resistance.

When you have the right feel, take the pork out and open the foil to vent it. The bark may have softened – don't worry, it will firm up as you vent. I vent for about half an hour, then re-wrap the pork, place a towel over it and let it rest for another hour.

Then, it's time to get your pull on. The meat should come apart easily. Cut off that money muscle and set aside for slicing rather than shredding. On the opposite side of the butt to the money muscle is the horn muscle, under the paddle bone. Whip this out and put it with your money muscle.

Now get pulling! Place the butt and the foil juices in a large tray and get going. Try not to shred it too fine. Remove the scapula, and throw away any fat seams. Finally, add the remainder of your foil marinade and toss the pork through. You're good to go.

At the Grillstock festivals 2015, Stephen Heyes competed as his alter ego Priscilla Queen of the Firepit, raising thousands of pounds for the charity Mind.

AND THAT IS PRETTY MUCH IT – COMPETITION PORK, JEDI-STYLE.

@JediSwineTricks

www.jediswinetricks.com

BACKYARD-STYLE PORCHETTA

Porchetta is an old-school Italian recipe – the meat would originally have been cooked over fire or in a pizza oven. Imagine a huge 10kg porchetta coming out of a wood oven – in itself a reason for a village celebration, for families and friends to get together, particularly with the pig being such a prized beast and all. That's exactly what we're all about, too.

Porchetta is ace to cook over wood or coals. The burning wood gives a tasty char to the crispy crackling and a heady kick of flavour to the succulent, juicy meat. It's what it should be.

Our porchetta consists of a pork belly wrapped around a whole pork loin. Pork belly is awesome and we think pretty much anything wrapped in one and cooked for a few hours will taste good. But wrap a whole pork belly around more pork? That's the stuff dreams are made of. It's a bit costly and fiddly, but you'll feed a whole load of folk and you'll be dining out on the glory for months to come.

FEEDS 12–16

INGREDIENTS

3-4kg pork belly, about 40cm x 25cm and 4cm thick

50g sea salt flakes, preferably Maldon

100g fresh fennel tops, finely chopped

2 tbsp fennel seeds

2 tbsp finely chopped rosemary

2 tbsp finely chopped thyme leaves

2 tbsp finely chopped sage leaves

8 garlic cloves, minced

finely grated zest of 1 orange

finely grated zest of 1 lemon

2 tsp freshly ground black pepper

2 tsp fine sea salt

2-4kg boneless pork loin (the same length as the pork belly)

Braised Fennel (see p.179) or Chimichurri (see p.195), to serve

METHOD

① Pat dry the pork belly, then score the skin in a criss-cross pattern, making cuts about 1cm deep and 2cm apart. (See photographs, over the page.)

② Mix together the salt flakes, fennel tops, fennel seeds, herbs, garlic, orange and lemon zest and pepper in a bowl, setting aside the fine sea salt for later.

③ Flip the pork belly over, meat-side up, stab it all over with a knife and rub the herby spice mix on top. Wrap tightly in cling film and leave in the fridge for a minimum of 1 hour or a day or two, if you have time.

④ Remove the pork from the fridge about 1 hour before you plan to start cooking to let it come up to room temperature.

⑤ Place the pork loin on top of the belly to one side. Wrap the belly around the loin. Secure with kitchen string, tying it at 2.5cm intervals.

⑥ Sprinkle the skin of the belly with the reserved fine salt.

⑦ Set up your BBQ to cook directly (see p.18) at a medium heat, around 150°C. If you have a rotisserie attachment, attach your porchetta to it.

⑧ Cook the porchetta for about 2½ hours, turning it often, until the skin is crisp with a lovely dark bark. The internal temperature should hit 75°C.

⑨ Remove the pork from the BBQ and leave it to rest for 10 minutes. Serve sliced with braised fennel or chimichurri.

PIG CHEEKS

A long-time secret favourite of chefs and butchers alike, pit-smoked pig cheeks are like regular pulled pork dialled up to 11. They are an intense, gelatinous, uber-rich and pumped-up sticky piggy treat that falls apart in the mouth. We love them.

They're not huge – one cheek is about the size of a small plum – so you need a few per person for a decent-sized portion. Then, you pit-braise them – they are cooked inside the smoker in a tray with a little liquid for some of the time.

FEEDS 4

INGREDIENTS

12 pig cheeks, about 200g each

Grillstock House Rub (see p.202)

500ml cider

Backyard BBQ Sauce (see p.194)

The rest

4 Tom Herbert's Buns (see p.168), split and lightly toasted

Damn Fast Awesome Pickles (see p.178)

METHOD

① Liberally season the pig cheeks all over with the rub. Leave the cheeks for 1 hour to come up to room temperature.

② Set up your BBQ for smoking (see p.19), around 110°C. Add your choice of smoking wood to the coals.

③ Put the pig cheeks directly onto the grill bars and cook for around 3 hours, then arrange them in a foil tray in an even layer.

④ Pour half the cider into the tray. Drink the other half. Cover the tray with foil and return it to the BBQ to cook for a further 2 hours or until the internal temperature hits 92°C.

⑤ Remove the cheeks from the foil tray, discard the braising liquid and put them directly on the grill. Brush the cheeks with the BBQ sauce and cook for another 10 minutes or until caramelized.

⑥ Tear the cheeks into large chunks and pile into the buns with pickles.

PIG CHEEKS ARE GREAT SERVED WITH A SIDE OF COLLARD GREENS (SEE P.190) HEAVILY DOUSED IN JALAPEÑO VINEGAR (SEE P.200) TO CUT THROUGH THE RICHNESS.

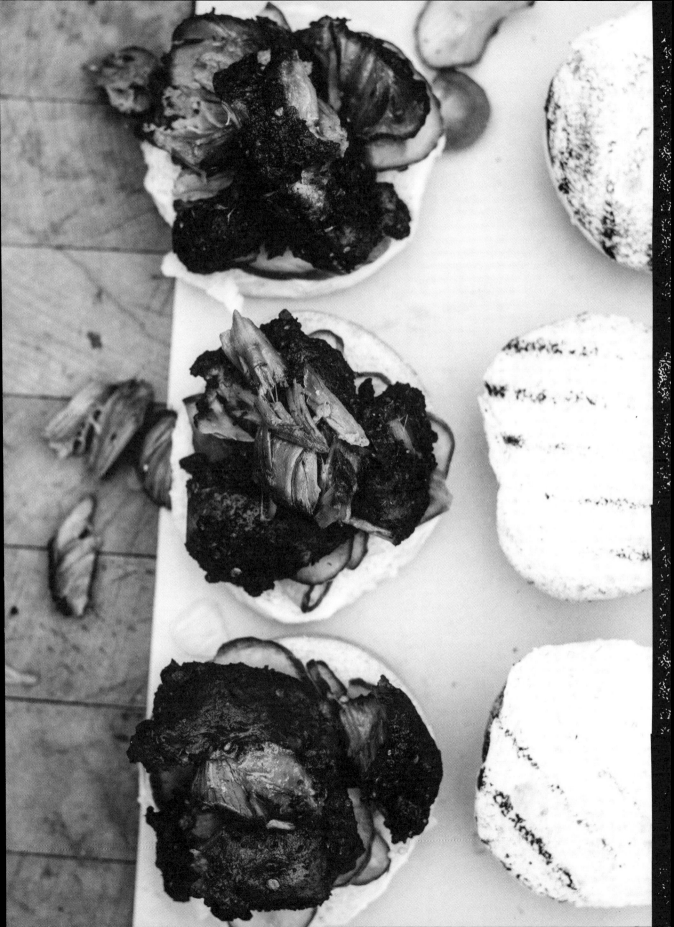

BUTTERFLIED STUFFED TENDERLOINS

Pork tenderloins are pretty lean and, dare we say, a little bland on their own. You can rev them up with a good, punchy BBQ rub, but they also lend themselves to being stuffed to pack in extra flavour.

Select the chunkiest pork tenderloins you can find — it will make stuffing them that much easier.

FEEDS 6

INGREDIENTS

300g jar of roasted peppers, drained and roughly chopped

100g soft goat's cheese

2 pork tenderloins, about 400g each

Grillstock House Rub (see p.202)

METHOD

① Set up your BBQ to cook indirectly (see p.19) at a medium heat, around 170°C.

② Mix the peppers and goat's cheese together until combined.

③ To prepare the pork, make a horizontal cut along one side of each tenderloin, stopping 2cm from the far edge so the two halves remain attached. Open out the pork like a book and cover it with cling film. Using the palm of your hand, gently flatten the loins until about 1cm thick. Trim any scraggy edges.

④ Lightly dust both sides of the loins with the rub.

⑤ Place the opened-out loins horizontally on a work surface. Spread the stuffing over the bottom two-thirds of each loin, about 1cm thick. From the bottom up, roll the pork tightly, taking care not to squeeze the stuffing out. Secure with kitchen string, tying it at 2.5cm intervals.

⑥ Put the pork on the BBQ and cook for 30 minutes, turning the loins every 10 minutes until nice and golden all over and cooked through. The internal temperature should hit 70°C.

⑦ Remove the string and slice into rounds to serve.

Instead of the pepper-and-goat's-cheese stuffing, you could try:

• your favourite sausage meat

• a combo of slices of provolone cheese, fresh spinach and prosciutto ham

• leftover Smokehouse Pulled Pork (see p.29)

Or (as it goes) whatever else you fancy...

PORK CHOP T-BONES

Pork chop T-bones often get overlooked in favour of their bigger, beefier cousins. But actually they are cheaper and every bit as flavoursome and juicy. As with a good steak, try to buy your pork chops directly from your butcher and have them cut to just how you like them. In this case you should like them about 3cm thick so that a good, tasty char can build up on the outside, while the middle stays juicy and tender. Serve the T-bones cooked to medium – long gone are the days when you need to be scared of serving pork a little pink. Treat them like steak and you will be rewarded with porky delights.

FEEDS 4

INGREDIENTS

4 centre-cut T-bone pork loin chops, each about 3cm thick

Grillstock House Rub (see p.202)

METHOD

① Liberally season the pork chops all over with the rub. Leave them for 1 hour to come up to room temperature.

② Set up your BBQ to cook directly (see p.18) at a medium heat, around 180°C.

③ Put the chops on the BBQ and cook for 10-12 minutes, turning them every 2 minutes, until the internal temperature hits 65°C for medium.

④ Loosely cover the chops with foil and leave to rest for 10 minutes before serving.

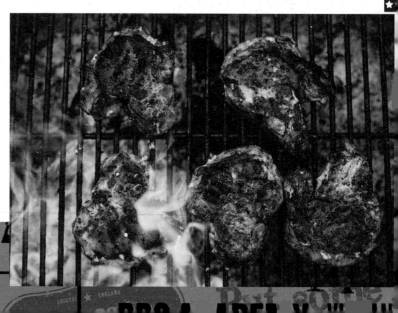

HOMEMADE BACON

Bacon. Just saying the word out loud sends a shiver down the spine. The senses become aroused and the pulse starts to race. Palms start to sweat and now all you can think about is bacon. And more bacon. Go on, say it again. Bacon. Now whisper it slowly like you're about to make sweet, sweet love to it... shhh... gently now... baaaaaaacon...

No food on the entire planet captures the imagination like bacon. It goes with *everything* and people do some crazy stuff with it – bacon straws, bacon ice cream, bacon weaves, bacon roses, bacon jam, bacon taco shells, even a bacon unicorn horn. We've seen bacon air-fresheners, bacon lip balm and bacon aftershave. There are entire cookbooks written just about bacon. People don't just 'love' bacon. It's beyond that. It's emotional.

The problem is that most bacon you buy is let down by processing. You start with a glorious pork belly and the end result falls short of its true potential. We've all slung a couple of rashers into a pan and wondered where all that water comes from. We don't want our bacon sloppy, flabby, grey and limp. Something must be done.

FEEDS 8–10

INGREDIENTS

150g coarse sea salt, preferably Maldon

2 tbsp light soft brown sugar

1kg pork belly, skin on, patted dry

ketchup, to serve

METHOD

① Mix together the salt and sugar (this is the salt cure), then rub the mixture all over the pork.

② Put the pork in a large zip-lock bag and tip in any leftover salt/sugar mixture. Squeeze out the air and seal the bag tightly.

③ Place the bag in a plastic tray at the bottom of the fridge for 5 days, turning and massaging the bacon every day. If you like, you can invent a little bacon song and dance to perform while you do this. We believe it makes better bacon...

④ When the 5 days are up, remove the bacon and rinse well. Discard everything else.

⑤ Pat the bacon dry with kitchen paper and leave on a wire rack in a cool, well-ventilated place to dry out for a day or two. Protect the bacon with a sheet of muslin while it's drying.

⑥ After drying, slice to the perfect bacon-slice thickness and grill over a direct medium–high heat, turning occasionally, until cooked to your liking. Ketchup for dunking is a must.

BE HAPPY IN THE KNOWLEDGE YOU HAVE CREATED THE ULTIMATE FOOD. OMG... BEST... BACON... EVER.

HOW TO FLAVOUR YOUR BACON

All BBQ guys like to tinker. No sauce is ever perfect and every rub is always in BETA mode. Well, homemade bacon is the same. We like to find reasons to spend a day at the grill, standing around eating pork products. Experimentation in flavouring your own homemade bacon stacks up as a day well spent.

TREACLE-FLAVOURED BACON

Our butcher, Paul, loves his bacon cured with some treacle. Frankly, he'd eat your shoe if you covered it in treacle, but it does work well with the cure. Try adding 2-3 tbsp treacle to the salt-cure mix then carry on the recipe as described on the previous page. The treacle turns the bacon a beautiful colour, too.

MAPLE-FLAVOURED BACON

A lovely option is to add 2-3 tbsp maple syrup to the cure for the classic maple sweet-cure bacon.

JUNIPER & PEPPER-FLAVOURED BACON

Try adding 2 tbsp each of crushed juniper berries and black pepper-corns to the salt-cure mix.

BBQ-RUB-FLAVOURED BACON

Add 50g of your favourite BBQ rub to the salt-cure mix to make things a little more interesting.

EASTERN-FLAVOURED BACON

Give your bacon a fancy, exotic twist by adding 2 tbsp Chinese 5-spice to the salt-cure mix, along with a shot or two of your choice of hot sauce.

COLD-SMOKED BACON

Cold smoking your cured bacon is awesome. Powdered wood in a smoke box at the bottom of your BBQ works well. Cold smoke it after the cure, but before the resting and drying time, while the surface is a little moist and sticky. This will help the smoke stick.

'LIFE EXPECTANCY WOULD GROW BY LEAPS AND BOUNDS IF GREEN VEGETABLES SMELLED AS GOOD AS BACON.'

Doug Larson, columnist

PORK
★ RIBS ★

GRILLSTOCK SMOKEHOUSE BABY BACK RIBS

Baby backs are great to cook. They're usually easier to get hold of than their bigger cousins – spare ribs – and because they're smaller, they require less time on the smoker, too. Baby backs work well with a sweet, almost candied coating – so feel free to add a bit more sugar to your house rub, if you like.

FEEDS 4

INGREDIENTS

4 racks baby back ribs, about 350g each

Grillstock House Rub (see p.202)

300ml Backyard BBQ Sauce (see p.194)

House Slaw (see p.184), to serve

METHOD

① First, remove the tough membrane from the ribs (see box, right). Trim off any excess fat or scraggy bits of meat to give a clean, neat rack.

② Liberally season the ribs all over with the rub. Leave them to stand for at least 30 minutes to come up to room temperature.

③ Set up your BBQ for smoking low 'n' slow (see p.19), around 110°C. Add your choice of smoking wood to the coals – we like to use pecan or fruit wood such as apple, pear or cherry with ribs.

④ Put the ribs on the BBQ, bone-side down, and smoke for 4 hours or until the internal temperature hits 92°C. The ribs are ready when the meat comes away from the bone when pulled, but is not falling off the bone.

⑤ Brush the meaty side of the ribs with the BBQ sauce and cook for a further 15 minutes until golden and caramelized.

⑥ To serve, flip the racks of ribs meat-side down and slice between each bone.

⑦ Serve with a big bowl of slaw.

To remove the membrane on the bony side of a rack of ribs (don't skip this part – it's important), take the end of a blunt knife and tease away a membrane edge from the bone, so you can get hold of it. Using kitchen paper for grip, pull away gently. You'll probably need a few goes at it before it comes away fully.

ST. LOUIS SPARE RIBS

When most people think of perfect 'last meal' BBQ, it's a pile of ribs like these.

St. Louis ribs start off as a full sheet of spare ribs with the bottom, gristle rib tips sliced off and the small, scraggy end bit of the rack removed to leave a beautifully straight, rectangular, uniform rack of ribs.

They're bigger than baby back ribs (see p.52), so they take a bit longer on the smoker, but it's worth every extra second for big mouthfuls of smoky, succulent, delicious, sweet meat.

You're not looking for the meat to fall off the bone – in fact, you'd lose points in competition for that. You want some chew, to retain some bite and texture, and for the meat to come away cleanly.

People seem divided on whether or not to remove the membrane from spare ribs, but we believe it is an absolute MUST DO – even if it is a pain in the ass. Finally, if you're short on time for rib cooking, check out the 3-2-1 Texas Crutch Method on page 56.

FEEDS 4

INGREDIENTS

2 racks of spare (belly) ribs, St. Louis-cut trimmed, about 1.25kg each

Grillstock House Rub (see p.202)

Backyard BBQ Sauce (see p.194)

METHOD

1 First, remove the tough membrane from the ribs (see box, p.52). Trim off any excess fat or scraggy bits of meat to give a clean, neat rack.

2 Liberally season the ribs all over with the rub. Leave them to stand for 1 hour or so while they come up to room temperature.

3 Set up your BBQ for smoking low 'n' slow (see p.19), around 110°C. Add your choice of smoking wood to the coals – we like to use pecan or fruit wood such as apple, pear or cherry with ribs.

4 Put the ribs on the BBQ, bone-side down, and smoke for 7 hours or until the internal temperature hits 88°C. The ribs are ready when the meat comes away from the bone when pulled, but is not falling off. If they're not there yet, open another beer and wait 45 minutes before checking again.

5 When the ribs reach 88°C, brush the meaty side with BBQ sauce and cook for 10-15 minutes until dark and sticky. To serve, flip them meat-side down and slice between each bone. Pile them up for eating.

THE TEXAS CRUTCH METHOD

If you're short on time for cooking your spare ribs, the 3-2-1 Texas Crutch Method brings the overall time in the smoker down to a mere six hours. Barely enough cooking hours to open a beer and get comfortable.

This is a technique that started out on the competition circuit as a way to save pitmasters who were worried about time, or concerned about their ribs drying out before the all-important turn-in time to the judges' table.

It's pretty rare now to see competition cooks that don't use the Texas Crutch Method — it's everywhere and it has made its way into backyard cooking, too.

If you have good meat and plenty of time, there's really no reason to bother, but if you want to speed your cooking up a bit, then it works well. The idea is to give your ribs a good three hours in the smoke to pick up colour and flavour.

Then, you lay out a double layer of industrial-strength foil, twice as long as your rib rack, and place your part-cooked ribs on top of it, at one of the short ends. You can stack two racks on top of one another on the foil, if you have them. Then, drizzle the ribs with honey or sprinkle with a little brown sugar, if you like.

Fold over the free end of the foil and crimp up the sides, nice and tight, leaving an opening at the top. Before you completely seal the ribs in the foil pouch, add a slosh of apple juice or cider.

Place the fully sealed foil pouch back on the smoker for a couple of hours. This is the 'Texas Crutch', which essentially steams and braises the rib meat, keeping it succulent and speeding up the cooking process.

After about 2 hours, take the ribs out of the foil pouch and place them back on the smoker for a final hour. 3-2-1 simple.

TEXAS CRUTCH IN A NUTSHELL
- 3 HOURS IN THE SMOKE
- 2 HOURS IN THE FOIL POUCH
- 1 HOUR BACK IN THE SMOKE

CHARLIE AND GEMMA – TEAM SMOKIN' PENGUIN –
ARE TWO OF THE NICEST (AND THIRSTIEST) FOLK IN
THE COMPETITION BBQ WORLD. ENOUGH SAID.

★ TEAM SMOKIN' PENGUIN'S ★
— RIBS —

FEEDS 8

INGREDIENTS

a couple of racks of extra-meaty
spare ribs

250g butter

maple syrup

RIB RUB

10 tbsp dark soft brown sugar

4 tbsp decent salt

2 tbsp ground coriander

1 tbsp Coleman's mustard powder

2 tbsp onion powder

2 tbsp sweet paprika

4 tsp garlic powder

4 tsp freshly ground black pepper

1 tsp chipotle powder

RIB SAUCE

500ml sweet BBQ sauce

small tin of pineapple chunks in
juice - blitzed to a smooth purée

125g butter

RIB JUICE

250ml peach nectar

250ml red grape juice

125ml cider vinegar

125ml maple syrup

60ml Worcestershire sauce

2 tbsp rib rub

METHOD

In spite of what you may have
heard from David Attenborough
(yes, we see you with your creepy
penguin robots - we're not falling
for it, just distracting you from
our bad-ass outdoor kitchen),
us penguins aren't just fans of
fish - we bloody love meat! After
a long day of sliding about,
keeping eggs warm and distracting
film crews, there's nothing quite
like a rack of ribs or two.

But, let's start with the
important bit - a decent drink.
When we're cooking piggy goodness,
we like our own twist on a
classic - perfectly matched and
tasty as hell: the Rib Roy! Start
with 50ml of a decent bourbon, or
a rye if you're feeling fruity.
Chuck that into a Boston shaker
full of ice with 25ml of vermouth
- something classy but not too
sweet, like a Punt e Mes. Hold
onto your horses, or sea lions,
this is where it gets cray-cray
(read this with the irony it
deserves). Add a teaspoon of peach
nectar and ¼ teaspoon of maple
syrup. Stick the lid on and shake
the thing like it's been bad and
you need to teach it a lesson!
It's ready when there's a frosting
to the outside of your shaker.
Strain and serve straight up,
garnished with a slice of bacon.

With the hard part out the way,
it's time to cook some meat. First,

the meat. Make friends with the best butcher in town. Well-looked-after pigs are generally the tastiest pigs. If your pig has lived in a 20-room mansion, dining at the Fat Duck and listening to Vivaldi, he'll be nicer to your taste buds than if he's lived in a council flat, with Sky TV and a dog on a string. Find a great butcher, ask him about the meat, discuss the cuts you're after and ask him for a decent rack of ribs with a fair bit of meat on each bone!

We trim our ribs St. Louis style. It's up to you if you want to do this, but we think it makes for a better-looking rib, removes any chance of getting a bit of cartilage in your mouth and isn't too hard to do - it's even easier if you get your local butcher to do it, but in the UK he may look at you blankly, then try to sell you a pork pie.

To do the St. Louis cut yourself, lay the ribs flat, meat-side up. Find the smallest rib at one end and trim it off with a straight cut between that rib and the one next to it. This'll remove the straggly meat that's gonna cook too fast. Do the same to the other end. Next, find the longest rib. Feel up to the end nearest the breast plate at the top: you'll feel a lump of bone, then a softer bit. Using a decent knife, slice perpendicular to the ribs and follow that line all the way along, cutting through the soft bit on each rib (where it meets the breast bone). You'll see small, white circles at the top of each rib when you look at it side on.

Flip your ribs meat-side down to see if your butcher's left the membrane on the back of them. Cooked, this turns into a nasty rubbery nightmare; the sort of thing that men in black suits with dark glasses use to make you confess to things you haven't done!

To get this off, use a blunt butter knife and ease it under the membrane at the cut end of the bones. Easy tiger... Once you've got a little bit up, grab the slippery beggar with some kitchen towel and have it away - then throw it in the bin, burn the bin, bury the ashes and salt the ground. Trim any thick, fatty bits on the ribs.

Get your smoker to a stable 110°C. A couple of hours before you cook, rub your meat. Grab the rub ingredients and give them a good mix together in a bowl. Make sure there are no clumps.

Apply that rub liberally - cover your meat in rubby goodness and then stick the ribs in the fridge. I wouldn't recommend rubbing any earlier - the salt will start curing the ribs, giving them a bacony flavour. While bacon is the greatest discovery since moving

TO GET THIS OFF, USE A BLUNT BUTTER KNIFE AND EASE IT UNDER THE MEMBRANE AT THE CUT END OF THE BONES. EASY TIGER...

walkways in airports, it's not what we're looking for here.

With your smoker up to heat, throw the rack on, bones down, chuck a lump of your favourite wood (the correct answer is hickory) onto the coals, close the lid and kick back for 2½ hours. While you're relaxing, summon your manservant (get off your ass) to prepare the rib juice. The secret is to mix in a clockwise motion (OK, it doesn't make any difference, but I didn't want to make it seem so easy).

When the timer goes, pull out a length of foil about 1½ times the length of the rack and lay it flat. Down the centre, put a line of 1cm-thick butter slabs (use half a pack per rack - yep, butter's awesome!), then drizzle over maple syrup. Lay the rack meat-side down on the butter and bring up the sides of the foil. Pour ½-1 cup of the rib juice into the foil - you don't want it swimming, but you want enough. Seal up the foil and wrap another couple of layers around for luck. Now do the same with the other rack. Throw both racks back in the smoker.

You've got another wait on your hands - 2 hours this time. You could do some housework, or you could sit next to your smoker with a Rib Roy. About 1½ hours in, mix up the sauce ingredients, stick them in a foil tray and put that in the smoker to melt the butter. After another 30 minutes, grab one of the rib parcels. Open it and look at the ribs - the meat should have pulled back a bit from the bone. If you lift the ribs, they should start to tear apart. If they're not quite ready, they're not quite ready. Foil them back up and stick them back on - different pigs, different muscles. Think of the difference between a builder piggy and an office-worker piggy.

When the ribs are ready, open the foil and flip them meat-side up, stir your buttery sauce and paint it all over them. Close the foil and rest the ribs. After 15 minutes, open the foil in front of your mates and look like a bloody champ! When they're tucking in, sauce down their chins and love in their eyes, creep up behind them and whisper, 'A talking, walking, smokin' penguin taught me how to do this.'

@penguinbbq

www.teamsmokinpenguin.com

MEMPHIS-STYLE RIBS

While It's true that cooking plays a role in competition BBQ, sitting round a fire pit with your buddies, passing around a bottle of something or other and enthusiastically debating the best way to cook ribs plays a pretty big part, too.

One favourite topic is 'wet versus dry'. So, should ribs come sauced or should they come coated in nothing more than a dry-rub seasoning, the way they do in Memphis? Well, we like both ways, but if forced to make a choice, then perhaps Memphis-style just wins by a nose.

FEEDS 4-5

INGREDIENTS

2kg spare ribs, tough membrane removed (see box, p.52), and trimmed (see step 1, p.52)

Grillstock House Rub (see p.202)

white wine vinegar or cider vinegar, for spritzing

light soft brown sugar, for sprinkling

METHOD

(1) Prepare and cook the ribs in exactly the same way as the St. Louis Spare Ribs (see p.54) or the Grillstock Smokehouse Baby Back Ribs (see p.52) right up to the point where you sauce them. But instead of slathering with sauce, take a spritz bottle of white wine vinegar or cider vinegar and moisten the meaty side of the ribs.

(2) Now, lightly sprinkle the ribs with the sugar and a final generous dusting of house rub.

(3) To serve, flip the rack of ribs meat-side down and slice between each bone, then pile them up on a wooden board alongside your choice of sides.

BONELESS RIB MEAT SANDWICH

Paul, our butcher, brought a bunch of 'boneless ribs' in for us to play with one day. They're skinless pork belly meat taken off a sheet of spare ribs. It's like the meat you get on top of spare ribs, but without the bone. We love it. It cooks and tastes just like ribs, but is much easier to put in a sandwich. Less crunchy.

FEEDS 4

INGREDIENTS

4 pork belly squares, each about 12cm x 2cm thick, skin removed, leaving a 1cm layer of fat

Grillstock House Rub (see p.202)

The rest

4 Tom Herbert's Buns (see p.168), split and lightly toasted

House Slaw (see p.184)

Backyard BBQ Sauce (see p.194)

Damn Fast Awesome Pickles (see p.178)

METHOD

① Liberally season the pork belly squares all over with the rub. Leave them to stand for about 30 minutes to come up to room temperature.

② Set up your BBQ to smoke low 'n' slow (see p.19), around 110°C. Add your choice of smoking wood to the coals — we like to use pecan, hickory or fruit wood with pork.

③ Put the pork belly squares on the BBQ, fat-side up, and smoke for around 4 hours until most of the fat has rendered out and the meat can be pulled apart with your hands. The internal temperature should hit 92°C.

④ Now's the time to build your sandwiches, starting from the bottom up: bun, slaw, slab of pork belly, BBQ sauce, pickles, bun.

MAPLE-GLAZED MEATY RIBS

All the fun of spare ribs with the bonus of a fatty, sticky, thick slab of meaty deliciousness from the pork belly. You may need to order these ribs in advance from your butcher, trimmed to a rectangular shape. Cook them low 'n' slow – perfect for a day manning the coals with friends and a few beers.

FEEDS 4–5

INGREDIENTS

2kg sheet meaty ribs, tough membrane removed (see box, p.52), and trimmed (see step 1, p.52)

Grillstock House Rub (see p.202)

100ml apple juice

For the maple glaze

125g dark soft brown sugar

125ml bourbon

125ml soy sauce

125ml ketchup

125ml maple syrup

75ml honey

1 tbsp Frank's RedHot sauce

1 tbsp apple cider vinegar

METHOD

① Liberally season the prepared ribs all over with the rub. Leave them to stand for 4 hours to allow the rub to add flavour and the meat to tenderize.

② Set up your BBQ to smoke low 'n' slow (see p.19), around 110°C. Add your smoking wood to the coals – we like to use fruit wood or pecan with ribs.

③ Put the ribs on the BBQ, bone-side down, and smoke for 4 hours until the meat comes away from the bone when pulled, but it is not falling off.

④ Remove the ribs from the BBQ and place them on a large double-layered sheet of foil. Fold the foil over and crimp the sides to make a pocket. Pour in the apple juice and crimp the top. Return the ribs to the BBQ for 2 hours.

⑤ Remove the ribs from the foil and return them to the BBQ for 30 minutes or until the internal temperature hits 92°C.

⑥ While the ribs are on the final ascent to heavenly perfection, heat the ingredients for the maple glaze in a saucepan, stirring often. Brush the meaty side of the ribs with the glaze and cook for another 30 minutes, brushing with more glaze every 10 minutes until the ribs are dark and sticky. To serve, slice between each bone and pile them up on a tray.

BRISKET

SMOKEHOUSE BRISKET

In the world of competition BBQ, brisket separates the men from the boys. It's the hardest meat to get right. It starts off as tough as old boots, staying that way for hours until suddenly hitting the short window of 'Brisket Nirvana'. This perfect point of done-ness is when the fat and connective tissue have broken down, but not dried out. We want smoky, crisp bark, giving way to succulent, juicy, unctuous meat with a little bite. A perfect slice of brisket will have you uttering primeval noises usually reserved for the bedroom.

Even for Grand Champions, there's no surefire way to cook a perfect brisket. Selecting the biggest, fattiest, most marbled brisket you can find will give you the best start. Leave those scrawny, rolled-up excuses for meat for granny's Sunday pot roast. Buy big and plan for leftovers.

We cook brisket like they do in Texas with a simple salt-and-pepper-based rub, and served without any sauce.

FEEDS 10-12

INGREDIENTS

3-4kg whole beef brisket,
fat cap trimmed to 1cm thick

Beef Rub (see p.203)

The rest

Tom Herbert's Buns (see p.168)

One-hour Pickled Onions (see p.179)

House Slaw (see p.184)

METHOD

① An hour or so before you plan to start cooking, liberally season the beef all over with the rub. Leave the beef to come up to room temperature.

② Set up your BBQ for smoking (see p.19), around 110°C. Add your choice of smoking wood to the coals – we like to use oak, hickory and beech with beef.

③ Put the brisket on the BBQ, fat-side up, and smoke for around 6-7 hours or until the internal temperature hits around 85°C. This is when the fat and collagen break down, leaving you with beautifully tender, succulent and juicy brisket and a dark outer bark. By all means slice a bit off and test it at this point. Pitmaster's prerogative.

④ Once you've hit the magic 85°C, take the brisket off the BBQ. Cover loosely with foil and leave it to rest for 30 minutes. Do not skip this step.

⑤ Brisket dries out quickly once it's sliced, so wait until you're ready to serve before carving. Slice the brisket across the grain to around the thickness of a pencil. Save the meat juices to pour over the sliced beef.

⑥ Serve the brisket in or with a bun with pickled onions and slaw.

BRISKET BURNT ENDS

For us, burnt ends represent everything that is wonderful about BBQ. They are absolutely rammed with smoky, beefy, sticky, rich, seasoned flavour, but they can't be rushed. There are no short cuts, no ways to cheat. If you want to make great burnt ends, then you have to invest the time and love and first smoke a brisket (see p.70). You will be rewarded with meaty awesomeness.

We refer to burnt ends as 'nuggets of BBQ gold' in our Grillstock staff training, as well as on our menus. Made from the point section of a smoked brisket, a burnt end is the chunky, fattier part that sits on top of the flat. We use the flat for sliced brisket.

FEEDS 10 AS A SIDE

INGREDIENTS

1kg point section from Smokehouse Brisket (see p.70), fat trimmed, and cut into 2.5cm cubes

2 tbsp Grillstock House Rub (see p.202)

about 250ml Backyard BBQ Sauce (see p.194)

The rest

Damn Fast Awesome Pickles (see p.178)

Comeback Sauce (see p.200)

METHOD

① Put the cubes of smoked brisket in a foil tray and dust all over with the rub, being careful not to break up the meat.

② Set up your BBQ to cook indirectly (see p.19) at a low heat, around 110°C.

③ Pour the BBQ sauce over the smoked brisket and gently turn the meat until it is coated.

④ Put the tray on the BBQ and cook for 1 hour or until the meat starts to caramelize.

⑤ Remove the burnt ends from the BBQ and serve with pickles and Comeback Sauce.

RAY 'DR. BBQ' LAMPE IS BOTH OUR MENTOR AND OUR VERY CLOSE FRIEND.
I THINK HE'S TICKLING BEN IN THIS SHOT!

DR. BBQ'S
SMOKED
★ BRISKET FLAT ★
WITH MUCHO JALAPEÑOS

'This is a classic Texas combo all in one package. You can de-seed the jalapeños if you are a wimp or use habaneros if you are a bad-ass. I like the milder smoke of applewood, but go ahead and use a stronger wood if you like. But remember that if everyone is telling you the food is too smoky, it probably is. You as the cook are desensitized after standing in the smoke all day.' – Dr. BBQ

FEEDS 8

INGREDIENTS

2.25–2.7kg good-quality beef brisket flat

your favourite BBQ rub, as needed

2 tbsp olive oil

16 large jalapeños, chopped

sea salt

25ml beer

@DrBBQ

www.drbbq.com

METHOD

① Prepare your cooker to cook indirect at 110°C using medium applewood smoke for flavour. Season the brisket liberally with the BBQ rub.

② Cook the brisket fat-side down for 1 hour and then flip it to fat-side up. Cook for about another 3-4 hours until the internal temperature is 70°C.

③ Drizzle the oil over the jalapeños and season with salt. Toss to coat.

④ Lay out a big double layer of heavy-duty tin foil and add half of the jalapeño mixture. Top with the brisket, fat-side up, and then the remaining jalapeño mixture.

⑤ Pull up the sides of the foil and pour in the beer. Seal the parcel, taking care not to puncture the foil.

⑥ Return the brisket to the cooker. After another hour, check the internal temperature. When the brisket is tender to the poke of a fork, at an internal temperature of about 100°C, remove it from the cooker. Leave it to rest for 30 minutes, wrapped. Remove the brisket from the foil and strain the jalapeños. Slice the brisket across the grain, about 5mm thick, and serve it with the jalapeños.

HILLBILLY CHILLI

Rich, smoky and sumptuous take-your-time chilli – best cooked low 'n' slow in a cast iron pot in the embers of a fire or in a smoker. The smoke adds another wonderful layer of flavour.

FEEDS 6-8

INGREDIENTS

75g salted butter

2 large onions, chopped

4 garlic cloves, chopped

1kg leftover Smokehouse Brisket (see p.70), or 1kg stewing steak, cut into 2cm cubes

4 tbsp Chilli Seasoning (see p.206)

2 tbsp tomato purée

2 x 400g cans chopped tomatoes

2 shots bourbon (more, if you fancy)

6 tbsp black treacle

2 x 400g cans kidney beans, drained

500-750ml beef or chicken stock

salt and freshly ground black pepper

The rest

sour cream

Damn Fast Awesome Pickles (see p.178)

METHOD

① Set up your BBQ to cook indirectly (see p.19) at a low heat, around 110°C.

② Melt the butter in a large cast iron pan on the hob over a medium heat. Tip in the onions and garlic and cook for 5 minutes, stirring often, or until softened. Add the brisket and the chilli seasoning and stir until the meat is coated in the oniony spice mix.

If using stewing steak, remove the cooked onions and garlic from the pan and brown the steak for 5 minutes in batches. (You may want to add a splash of oil to prevent the butter burning.) Return the onions and garlic to the pan. Stir in the seasoning.

③ Add the tomato purée and chopped tomatoes, stir well, and bring almost to the boil. Turn down the heat and stir in the bourbon, treacle and beans before adding 500ml of the stock, and salt and pepper. Cover the pan with a lid and put it on the BBQ.

④ Taste after an hour or so to check the seasoning and chilli heat. It's better to adjust it at this point, rather than just before serving.

⑤ Cook for another 5 hours or so, stirring and adding more stock when needed. We're looking for a rich, glossy sauce with melt-in-the-mouth meat still in identifiable hunks. Serve the chilli topped with sour cream and pickles.

BURNT ENDS NACHOS

Admittedly, there are a few steps to making Burnt Ends Nachos. It's not a dish you can just decide to knock up when you get home from the pub.

First, you need to smoke your brisket (see p.70). Then from that you need to make your Brisket Burnt Ends (see p.74), then make your nacho cheese sauce. It's well worth the effort and the final assembly takes seconds.

You can swap out the burnt ends for pulled pork, if you like. Or a mixture of the two. Or, if you're feeling particularly filthy, use Hillbilly Chilli (see p.78) in place of the burnt ends – but make sure you have plenty of face wipes.

FEEDS 4

INGREDIENTS

4 large handfuls of plain tortilla chips

300g Brisket Burnt Ends (see p.74)

Backyard BBQ Sauce (see p.194)

150ml sour cream

pickled or fresh jalapeño chilli peppers, sliced

For the nacho cheese sauce

2 tbsp unsalted butter

2 tbsp plain flour

500ml whole milk, warmed

100g mature Cheddar cheese, grated

100g pecorino or manchego cheese, grated

100g Monterey Jack, Gouda or Edam cheese, grated

a splash of Frank's RedHot sauce

salt and freshly ground black pepper

METHOD

① To make the nacho cheese sauce, melt the butter in a saucepan over a medium heat. Reduce the heat, add the flour and cook for 2 minutes, stirring continuously, until you achieve a smooth paste.

② Gradually whisk in the milk and bring the sauce to simmering point. Cook the sauce for 5-10 minutes, stirring continuously, until it thickens to the consistency of double cream.

③ Stir the cheeses into the sauce until melted. Add a splash of hot sauce and season with salt and pepper. Now, you're ready to assemble the nachos.

④ Spread the tortilla chips out evenly on a large plate, dish or wooden board.

⑤ Distribute the burnt ends over the chips.

⑥ Drizzle over the nacho cheese sauce – be generous.

⑦ Next, drizzle over the Backyard BBQ Sauce.

⑧ Then it's the sour cream's turn.

⑨ Finish off with a scattering of jalapeños.

THE BUNCH OF SWINES BBQ TEAM HAS BEEN GRILLSTOCK
GRAND CHAMPION IN FIVE OUT OF THE TEN COMPETITIONS
WE'VE HAD SO FAR. THEY KICK BBQ ASS.

BUNCH OF SWINES'
GRILLSTOCK-WINNING
WAGYU BRISKET

★ ★

FEEDS 12-15

INGREDIENTS

5kg Wagyu brisket (a standard brisket will also work)

250g BoS Brisket Rub (see below)

250ml BoS Brisket Injection (see right)

200ml Brisket Love Foil Marinade (see right)

favourite BBQ sauce, to serve

BoS BRISKET RUB

(Mix all the ingredients together.)

70g salt

55g caster sugar

45g light soft brown sugar

35g paprika

1 tsp hot chilli powder

1 tsp ground cumin

1 tsp white pepper

2 tsp freshly ground black pepper

½ tsp cayenne pepper

1 tsp garlic powder

1 tsp onion powder

¼ tsp mustard powder

¼ tsp ground cinnamon

¼ tsp cocoa powder

BoS BRISKET INJECTION

(Mix the ingredients together in a pan, then warm them through slightly to help dissolve the Bovril. Chill before use.)

250ml beef stock

1 tbsp Bovril

BRISKET LOVE FOIL MARINADE

(Mix the ingredients together in a pan. Simmer the mixture for 5 minutes, but don't let it boil.)

250ml English ale (a porter or something rich like that)

50ml Worcestershire sauce

50ml vegetable oil

50ml cider vinegar

2 tbsp Bovril

2 tbsp favourite BBQ sauce

USING BOVRIL MIGHT SEEM STRANGE TO A LOT OF PEOPLE, BUT BOVRIL IS AN UMAMI ENHANCER, WHICH WILL HELP ADD EXTRA DEPTH AND SAVOURY NOTES TO THE BRISKET.

METHOD

We always use Wagyu beef when competing at the Grillstock festivals — it has given us some great results. Wagyu is a Japanese cow breed, which is given beer and fed on a diet designed to produce a higher fat content in comparison to other beef. This extra fat lends itself very well to this type of BBQ, as it'll have less chance of drying out when we're cooking for 12 hours, while also giving a rich, buttery flavour.

Before you can start cooking a competition-style brisket, you'll need to know the different parts of the brisket and how they're going to cook. A brisket is made up of two muscles — the point and the flat. The flat is the leaner part of the brisket, which we use for slices; the point is a lot more marbled — we cube this up and use it for burnt ends. First, find exactly where the point and the flat are on your brisket so that you trim the correct side.

Once you've got the brisket flat-side up, trim off the excess fat and silver skin attached to it, as this will otherwise stop the rub sticking and smoke getting into the meat on this side. Then, start to semi-separate the point from the flat. Use a knife to slice along the fat seam between the point and flat and start to separate it, but leave it attached.

This is to allow you to expose more of the surface of the point to get more rub onto it. We leave

all of the fat on the back of the brisket to help protect the brisket from the heat — it's also much easier to remove from the brisket once it's cooked.

Once you've trimmed up the brisket, you want to place it into a large foil tray and start injecting the brisket using 250ml of injection mixture. Work across the brisket, injecting with the grain every 2.5cm with 5ml of the injection each time. Once you've gone over the flat, inject two full syringes into the point and then wipe away any excess injection with a piece of kitchen roll.

Apply dry rub onto the brisket and then let the rub melt into the meat for about 2-3 hours.

While the rub is setting on the brisket, you can go and set up your smoker. You're aiming for a cooking temperature of 110°C.

Once your smoker is up to temperature, put the brisket on as close to your thermometer as possible and then add a mix of cherry and hickory woods and smoke for 7 hours. Just before the brisket has been on the smoker for 7 hours, lay out two long pieces of extra-thick foil, each 2½ times the length of the brisket. Take

FIRST, FIND EXACTLY WHERE THE POINT AND THE FLAT ARE ON YOUR BRISKET SO THAT YOU TRIM THE CORRECT SIDE.

TEST THE MEAT FOR TENDERNESS - IT SHOULD BE LIKE PROBING A BLOCK OF WARM BUTTER.

the brisket out of the smoker and place it on one half of the foil, then check that you can get the other half to fold over the top of it. Fold and crimp the long side of the foil furthest away from you, place a temperature probe in the centre of the flat, pour 200ml of the foil marinade over the top of the brisket and close up the remaining sides of the foil. Place the brisket back into the smoker and cook 'til you hit 100°C.

Test the meat for tenderness - it should be like probing a block of warm butter. Once it's ready, take the meat off the smoker, bring it back into the kitchen and open the foil to allow the brisket to vent and to stop it cooking any further. Once the meat has vented for 5 minutes, wrap the foil back up tightly around it and allow it to rest for a minimum of 30 minutes.

When you're ready to serve, slide a long knife between the point and the flat to remove the point, and then slice the point up into cubes. With the flat, flip it over so all of the fat that we left on the bottom of the brisket is showing and remove this with a knife. Flip the flat back over and slice the brisket across the grain into 5mm slices. Serve with your favourite BBQ sauce.

@bunchofswines

www.bunchofswines.com

'We've been competing in American BBQ contests since 2011 and have competed in some of the largest and most prestigious contests across Europe and the USA, such as Grillstock, the American Royal in Kansas City and the Jack Daniel's World BBQ Championship. Brisket has been one of our strongest categories over the years. In our second-ever contest, we won the category and, when it comes to brisket, have gone on to establish ourselves as one of the teams to beat.' - Bunch of Swines

BREAKFAST BRISKET HASH

Brisket is the meat that just keeps on giving. It's always worth smoking a whole brisket even if you're feeding only a few people, just for the meals you'll get out of the leftovers. And there's nothing wrong with BBQ for breakfast in our book. This recipe makes enough to send four hungry people into their day with a spring in their step. You could swap the brisket for pulled pork, but we prefer brisket for breakfast.

FEEDS 4

INGREDIENTS

4 tbsp vegetable or sunflower oil

4 large potatoes, peeled and cut into 1cm cubes

1 onion, diced

1 green pepper, deseeded and diced

1 red pepper, deseeded and diced

500g leftover Smokehouse Brisket (see p.70) or Smokehouse Pulled Pork (see p.29), cubed, chopped or pulled

2 tbsp Grillstock House Rub (see p.202)

The rest

smoked streaky bacon rashers

8 eggs

a splash of Frank's RedHot sauce (optional)

METHOD

① Heat the oil in a large, heavy-based frying pan over a medium heat. Add the potatoes and cook for about 15 minutes, moving them around the pan every few minutes so they don't stick, until browned all over and almost cooked through.

② Toss in the onion and peppers and cook for another 5 minutes, turning often, until softened.

③ Add the brisket and rub to the pan and cook for a few more minutes, until heated through and golden and crisp in places.

④ While the hash is cooking, fry or grill your bacon until golden and crisp.

⑤ Just before you're ready to serve, fry up a couple of eggs per person.

⑥ To serve, top the hash with the bacon and eggs or you can add the bacon and eggs once you've piled up the hash on individual plates, if you prefer.

⑦ Finish this meaty feast with a splash or two of Frank's RedHot sauce, if you fancy.

BONE BROTH-DIPPED ★ ★
BRISKET ROLL ★ ★ ★

Brisket tends to dry out a little bit once you've cooked it and left it overnight, so here's a top way to use up some leftovers and get it nice and juicy again.

The dipping technique is like dunking a digestive biscuit in a mug of tea – long enough so it goes soft, wet and lovely, but not so long that it disintegrates, slips under the surface and sinks to the bottom. Timing is crucial. Be alert. And make sure you have lots of serviettes.

FEEDS 4

INGREDIENTS

600g Smokehouse Brisket (see p.70), fresh from the smoker or wrapped in foil and gently reheated if using leftovers

4 Tom Herbert's Buns (see p.168), split

For the beef bone broth
(makes 1.5–2 litres)

1.5kg leftover beef bones (ask your butcher, who'll probably give them to you for free)

2 tbsp black peppercorns

1 carrot

1 celery stick

1 onion, halved

a splash of cider vinegar

3 bay leaves

METHOD

① Set up your BBQ to cook indirectly (see p.19) at a high heat, around 200°C. If you want to add smokiness to the broth, add some wood chunks at this point.

② To make the beef bone broth, put the bones on the BBQ and roast for around 1 hour, turning them occasionally.

③ Transfer the bones to a deep roasting tray or a heatproof dish that fits your BBQ. Add the rest of the broth ingredients, then pour in about 3 litres water or enough to cover.

④ Close the vents of your BBQ to reduce the heat to 120°C and let the stock gently bubble away for a minimum of 6 hours, ideally 12 hours. You may need to skim off the fat occasionally.

⑤ Strain the broth into a bowl, discarding the solids, and use straightaway while still hot, or leave to cool before storing. You can store any leftover broth in the fridge, or freeze it if not using within 1 week.

⑥ Slice the brisket to around the thickness of a pencil and place in the buns.

⑦ Using a pair of tongs, dip the whole sandwich, bun and all, in the bowl of hot broth for a second or two. Serve the rolls with a small side bowl of extra broth for dunking.

CHRIS AND THE REST OF TEAM DIZZY PIG TOOK US IN LIKE FAMILY AT THE AMERICAN ROYAL IN KANSAS. THESE ARE GREAT GUYS WHO MAKE AWESOME RUBS.

DIZZY PIG'S
★ BEEF BRISKET ★

FEEDS 15–18

INGREDIENTS

6–8kg brisket

brisket injection (see below)

185g favourite beef rub (see method)

Brisket injection

500ml beef stock (the richer and beefier the better)

2 tbsp salt

1 tbsp MSG (optional)

METHOD

In order to impress the judges, many things have to come together, starting with the quality of the meat you are cooking with. We cook 'whole packer' briskets because BBQ is all about cooking big, honkin' pieces of meat! Plus, you'll want to give the judges meat from both of the main muscles in the brisket... the leaner flat and the fattier and luscious point. The flat is sliced to present, and the point is generally cut into bite-sized cubes. When selecting a brisket, choose one that has visible marbling of fat across the flat. As with most BBQ, the fattier the better! I like a brisket in the 6–8kg range, but as long as you have the whole brisket, you're ready to go.

TRIMMING

With a sharp knife, trim all of the membrane, silver skin, and globs of fat off of the top side of the flat. On the other side, you'll usually see a substantial layer of fat that covers the point, and part of the bottom of the flat. Trim the fat off the point muscle to expose the meat, but leave all the fat on where it covers the flat. That will protect it from the drying heat.

INJECTING

While it is not critical to inject your brisket, we like to get a little bit more flavour into the meat when cooking for competitions. The judge is going to take only a bite or two, so make it count. We like to use a mixture of beef stock and salt... and have been known to add some MSG. Using a purpose-made meat injector, load with liquid and pump the injection into the meat evenly, every 2.5cm-square or so.

SEASONING

Once your meat is injected, you are ready to season. The rub/ seasoning blend you use is an important part of the flavour of the final product, so make sure and use a seasoning that pairs nicely with beef, and has enough fresh spices to hold up to the long cook. The Dizzy Pig team has racked up over 70 brisket awards using nothing else but Dizzy Pig Cow Lick. It's a peppery blend that pairs perfectly with brisket, and has plenty of punch to hold up to the long cook and the robust flavour of beef. Season the brisket quite liberally on all sides. We typically use 185g Dizzy Pig Cow Lick on a 6-8kg brisket.

COOKING

There are many roads to cooking a good brisket, from low 'n' slow to hot and fast. I've settled in on the low side for my briskets, and 120-130°C is the pit temperature that works best for me. The key is to cook it until a tantalizing bark is formed on the outside as the seasoning, the smoke and the beef all combine to create a magical flavour. Most competition cooks, including us, like to give

the brisket some time wrapped in tin foil to enhance moisture and even out the cooking in this large piece of meat.

Prepare your smoker with charcoal and/or wood, and stabilize at 120-130°C. Ensure that your smoke is clean and sweet-smelling. The last thing you want is a strong, bitter smoke on your brisket. Use quality charcoal and dry wood, and give the fire time to burn cleanly. I use red oak, but hickory, maple, cherry and many other woods are excellent. Use what is available in your area, or your favourite.

Place the brisket on the cooker, fat-cap down and with the point end towards the hotter part of your cooker. Cook for about 8-10 hours until the brisket has formed a dark flavour crust, and is approximately 75-80°C at internal temperature. Double wrap it in tin foil, or place it in a covered pan.

Add about 125ml liquid... brewed coffee and beef stock are my choice. Return the tightly wrapped brisket to your smoker, and cook for 2-4 more hours.

Begin checking the tenderness when the internal temperature is 90°C. Your thermometer probe should slide in and out with little resistance. If it tugs back on you, wrap the brisket back up and check again in 20 minutes. Once the brisket is tender, remove it from the cooker, cover it with towels or a blanket and rest it for 1-3 hours before slicing.

@dizzypigbbq

www.dizzypigbbq.com

'In the BBQ world there's nothing better than biting into a perfectly cooked slice of beef brisket! Until you've tried it you'll just have to try and imagine the ultimate bold flavour that shouts BEEF more than any other cut on the cow. Well, the Dizzy Pig competition BBQ team has cooked a ton of briskets since they began competing professionally in 2002. Actually, when you do the math, it is over 2 tons. But the fact is Dizzy Pig racked up almost 70 top-ten brisket finishes in their first 120 contests (which includes eight trips to the American Royal Invitational, and seven invitations to the Jack Daniel's World BBQ Championship). Most folks agree, brisket is the most difficult BBQ category to cook consistently, and there is

a small window to hit in order to get a perfectly moist, tender and flavourful end result. But success can be achieved by:

• Choosing a quality whole brisket with good fat content

• Using a top-quality rub with a flavour that can stand up to the long cook

• Cooking with a good, clean-burning fire with the right amount of smoke

Don't forget, there are many roads that lead to a great bite of BBQ, so don't let anyone tell you there is only one way and you have to follow these steps. This is, of course, pure bullshit. There is some art involved, so you'll want to develop your own method that suits your cooker, your time frame, and your style.' - Dizzy Pig

CHICKEN

SIMPLE BBQ CHICKEN

If you're brand new to cooking low 'n' slow on your BBQ and you're looking for a recipe to kick off your new meaty hobby, this is the one. Smoking chicken is one of the easiest and tastiest things a man can do with a BBQ and some lumpwood.

Unless you have a smoker, the key to cooking good BBQ chicken is to set up your BBQ for two-zone cooking (see p.19). This gives you somewhere to move the chicken to before it burns, and allows it to cook through at its own pace. Take your time. Open another beer, relaxed in the knowledge that you're not the guy who burnt the chicken this year.

FEEDS 4

INGREDIENTS

2 chickens, quartered, about 1.3kg each (or the equivalent amount of chicken pieces)

Chicken Rub (see p.203)

Backyard BBQ Sauce (see p.194)

The rest

Potato Salad (see p.174)

Damn Fast Awesome Pickles (see p.178)

METHOD

① Set up your BBQ for two-zone cooking – the hotter, direct side (see p.18) at a medium heat, around 170°C. Add a solid handful of wood chunks to the coals.

Alternatively, you can smoke (see p.19) the chicken pieces, around 110°C. After step 2, put them on the smoker for a couple of hours until cooked through, then continue from step 5.

② Liberally season the chicken pieces all over with the rub.

③ Put the chicken pieces on the hotter, direct side of the BBQ and cook for 10-15 minutes, turning them often so they don't burn, until the skin is crispy all over.

④ Now move the chicken to the cooler, indirect side of the BBQ. Close the lid and smoke for 30-40 minutes or until the internal temperature hits 70°C. (If you want to get a bit fancy, spritz the top of the chicken with a mixture of apple juice and cider vinegar a couple of times as it cooks.)

⑤ Brush the chicken pieces with the BBQ sauce and continue to cook for a few more minutes until the skin caramelizes.

⑥ Serve the chicken with the potato salad and pickles.

COMPETITION CHICKEN WITH WHISKEY HONEY GLAZE

125ml soy sauce

125ml ketchup

60ml honey

2 tbsp Worcestershire sauce

1 tbsp Frank's RedHot sauce

1 tbsp cider vinegar

1 tsp Chicken Rub (see p.203)

When your friends come over for BBQ, they're looking for a good time. They want to eat your tasty meats, drink your cold beer, and hang out. While they're hoping your food will be succulent and delicious, they don't really care if your smoked chicken thighs don't look identical.

On the competition circuit, though, the judges really do care. You lose valuable points if the six thighs you turn in differ in any way. Pack your thighs tightly into a roasting tray to keep them uniform as they cook in all the seasoned juices.

FEEDS 4-6

INGREDIENTS

8-12 skin-on, bone-in chicken thighs

Chicken Rub (see p.203)

generous knob of salted butter

For the whiskey honey glaze

200g light soft brown sugar

125ml honey bourbon

METHOD

① Set up your BBQ to cook indirectly (see p.19) at a low heat, around 110°C.

② Mix together all the ingredients for the whiskey honey glaze in a saucepan. Bring to the boil, then turn the heat down and simmer for 10 minutes until thickened, stirring often.

③ While the glaze is simmering, liberally season the chicken all over with the rub.

④ Just before cooking, roll the thighs so the skin wraps around each one as much as possible. Pack them tightly together in a roasting tin, then dab a knob of butter on top of each thigh and sprinkle over more of the rub.

⑤ Put the thighs on the BBQ and cook for around 1½ hours or until browned and looking beautiful. The internal temperature should hit around 75°C.

⑥ Remove the thighs from the tin and place them directly on the grill. Smoke for a further 1 hour or until the skin starts to crisp.

⑦ Reheat the glaze, if needed. Dunk each thigh in the glaze until evenly coated, shake off any excess and then return to the grill for another 10-15 minutes until sticky and delicious. Serve your identical-looking thighs to impressed friends.

GRILLSTOCK ★2015★ PHOTO BOOTH

SMOKED BUFFALO WINGS

FEEDS 4

INGREDIENTS

16 2-joint chicken wings,
cut in half (mid and prime)

Chicken Rub (see p.203)

sprinkling of cayenne pepper
(optional)

For the wing sauce

4 tbsp Frank's RedHot sauce

4 tbsp melted butter

4 tbsp Backyard BBQ Sauce
(see p.194) (optional)

METHOD

① Set up your BBQ to cook directly (see p.18) at a medium heat, around 150°C.

Alternatively, after step 2, you can smoke (see p.19) the wings, around 110°C for about 2½ hours and finish them on a hot grill, until good and crispy (then continue with steps 4 and 5). This method will add a good layer of smoke flavour.

② Put the chicken wings in a large bowl, sprinkle with the rub and turn until thinly and evenly coated all over.

③ Put the wings on the BBQ and cook for 25–30 minutes, turning regularly, until browned and the internal temperature hits 75°C.

④ While the wings are cooking, make the wing sauce. Mix together the RedHot sauce and melted butter. You could also add the BBQ sauce, if you fancy.

⑤ Once the wings are cooked, toss them in a bowl with the sauce until evenly coated. For extra-hot wings, sprinkle with cayenne pepper before serving.

Wings are one of the staple man-food-style dishes. Us blokes love them.

It is widely believed that the original Buffalo wing was invented back in 1964 when Teressa Bellissimo, the owner of the Anchor Bar in Buffalo, NY, needed to knock up a late Friday-night snack for a group of hungry revellers. All that remained in the kitchen was a pile of chicken wings destined for the overnight stockpot. She fried them up, then slathered them with a spicy hot sauce. They've been on the menu at the Anchor Bar ever since.

We like to cook our Buffalo wings a little differently in the Smokehouse, sticking them in the hickory smoker to slow cook for a few hours before a quick dip in the fryer to crisp up the skin. This not only adds a lovely layer of smoky flavour, it also leaves the meat tender, delicious, juicy and succulent. We then toss the wings in our own Hot BBQ Sauce (see p.194).

Here's how to knock up some awesome wings at home using your regular BBQ.

HUEY AND THE FUN LOVIN' CRIMINALS SMASHED IT UP AT OUR BRISTOL FESTIVAL IN 2014. WE WELCOMED THEM BACK TO WALTHAMSTOW THE FOLLOWING YEAR.

HUEY'S FUN LOVIN
★ FRIED CHICKEN ★

1. Get yourself some chicken.

2. Prepare a bowl; get a big one so you don't make a mess.

3. Mix 2 fistfuls of cornflakes with 60g plain flour and one or two eggs. If it's too clumpy, throw a dash of olive oil in to smooth it out a little with a spoon. Don't use a blender!

4. Let that sit while you get choppin' - 2 cloves of garlic, slice 'em thin like Big Paulie from *Goodfellas* and fry them in a pan with some shallots, olive oil, and salt 'n' peppa, until the garlic and shallots are light brown.

5. Get the garlic and mix it with the cornflake/flour/egg stuff (batter).

6. I use chicken parts, but fillets are good too if you wanna make 'em into sandwiches. Get the chicken smeared with your batter from the big bowl.

7. Throw that on the grill or griddle, flip when you need to - cook thoroughly.

8. Eat the best damn chicken you ever made, Fun Lovin' Criminal-style.

SLICE 'EM THIN LIKE BIG PAULIE FROM *GOODFELLAS*

@OfficialHuey

#hueybook

www.funlovincriminals.co

BOURBON-BRINED SPATCHCOCK CHICKEN

Here's how to cook a chicken on the BBQ in far less time than it takes to roast one in the oven. It also overcomes the problem of the chicken being such an irregular shape that the breast meat is often overcooked by the time the leg and thigh meat are done – we give you moist and succulent meat throughout. Plus, you're cooking it over a fire, which is always more fun.

FEEDS 4

INGREDIENTS

1 chicken, about 1.8kg

Chicken Rub (see p.203)

For the brine

100ml bourbon

90g sea salt, preferably Maldon

90g light soft brown sugar

12 whole black peppercorns

METHOD

① To spatchcock the chicken, put it breast-side down on a chopping board with the legs towards you. Using poultry shears or a sharp knife, locate the backbone of the chicken and carefully cut down either side to remove it. Open out the chicken like a butterfly and turn it over. With the heel of your palm, flatten the breastbone so the chicken is roughly the same thickness all over.

② Brining the chicken is optional, but it gives a more succulent end result. If you're not brining, set up your BBQ to cook directly (see p.18) at a medium heat, around 160°C, then go to step 4.

③ To brine the chicken, pour 2 litres warm water into a large bowl. Add the rest of the brining ingredients and stir until dissolved. Leave to cool, then add the chicken, making sure it is submerged. Cover with cling film and refrigerate for 6 hours-ish. Remove the chicken from the brine and pat dry with kitchen paper. Discard the brine.

④ Before cooking, season the chicken all over with the rub.

⑤ Put the chicken, breast-side up, on the BBQ and cook for 20 minutes until the skin starts to turn crisp and golden. Turn the chicken over and cook for another 15–20 minutes or until cooked through.

We're aiming for an internal temperature of 75°C in the thickest part of the bird. If the skin starts to burn before the chicken is cooked, it is too close to the coals or your fire is too hot - in this case cook indirectly (see p.19) for the remaining cooking time.

⑥ Serve the chicken whole for everyone to help themselves.

BACON-WRAPPED STUFFED THIGHS

Whenever faced with the question 'How can I make this better?', the answer is usually 'Add bacon.' It certainly never makes things worse.

Here is a great recipe that you can prepare in advance of the crew coming round, bung on the BBQ for an hour or so, then sit back and accept the glory. It uses boneless chicken thighs so they're great to eat whole, too – good finger food. Kids love them.

FEEDS 6

INGREDIENTS

12 skinless, boneless chicken thighs

Chicken Rub (see p.203)

6 sausages, the meat squeezed out of the skins

24 streaky bacon rashers

Backyard BBQ Sauce (see p.194) (optional)

METHOD

① Set up your BBQ to cook indirectly (see p.19) at a low-medium heat, around 140°C.

② Open out the chicken thighs and lay them flat on a chopping board, the inside of the thighs facing upwards. Season lightly with the chicken rub - not too much as the bacon is quite salty.

③ Place a strip of sausage meat, about finger thickness, widthways across each thigh where the bone used to be. Roll the chicken thighs around the sausage meat, like a fat sausage roll.

④ Wrap rashers of streaky bacon around each chicken thigh parcel, about two per thigh. You can either wrap the thighs entirely in bacon or leave the ends showing. Dust the tops of the thighs with a little more rub.

⑤ Put the chicken thighs on the BBQ and cook for 1 hour until the bacon is crisp and golden and the internal temperature of each parcel hits 75°C.

You could dunk the thighs in Backyard BBQ Sauce 15 minutes before they're ready, if you like, and put them back on the grill to finish cooking until sticky and golden.

Jazz up the stuffing by mixing other ingredients into the sausage meat. Try freshly chopped chillies or cheese. Or more bacon. —

CHICKEN LOLLIPOPS

Meat that comes on its very own stick is our favourite of all the meats.

Chicken drumsticks lend themselves to this well. Usually, you hold onto the base of a drummer, but it can be a slippery, messy job. You have to cling to the oily, saucy skin as it slithers around on the bone. How are you supposed to have a good chew on that meat if you can't even grip it properly? This sort of thing upsets us, and keeps us awake at night.

The answer is to French trim – a method you usually see on racks of lamb ribs, where the bone part is trimmed right back of skin and fat until it is clean. It's easy to do to drumsticks, too. It looks fancy and everyone will love you for it. Pitmaster points right there.

FEEDS 4

INGREDIENTS

12 chicken drumsticks

Chicken Rub (see p.203)

Backyard BBQ Sauce (see p.194)

METHOD

① Set up your BBQ to cook directly (see p.18) at a medium heat, around 150°C.

Alternatively, after steps 2 and 3, you can smoke (see p.19) the drumsticks over an indirect heat, around 110°C, for about 2½ hours (then continue from step 5).

② To French trim the drumsticks, use a sharp knife to cut around each drumstick just below the main meaty part and through to the bone. Use your knife to scrape away and remove the skin and any cartilage until the end of the bone is clean.

③ Liberally season the chicken drumsticks all over with the rub.

④ Put the drumsticks on the BBQ and cook for 30-40 minutes, turning them often so they don't burn, until the internal temperature hits 75°C in the thickest part.

⑤ While the drumsticks are cooking, heat the BBQ sauce. Holding each drumstick by the bone, dunk into the sauce. Let the excess drip off, then return to the grill to cook over a gentle indirect heat for 10 minutes until golden all over.

CHEF'S CHOICE

BACON FATTY

Fatties are awesome. Several versions of them – bacon wraps stuffed with sausage meat and whatever else you fancy – have passed along the judges' table at our King of the Grill competitions, but this version is one of our favourites.

Fatties are also known as bombs. The bomb alternative, opposite, is a twist on the standard fatty. What the two versions have in common is a wrapping of crisp, golden streaky bacon. Bacon makes everything better. Fact.

FEEDS 2 AS A MAIN, OR 6 AS A SIDE

INGREDIENTS

14 thick streaky bacon rashers

5 traditional sausages, with the meat squeezed out of the skins

Grillstock House Rub (see p.202)

For the filling

choose from: grated mozzarella or other cheese, chopped chillies, shredded Smokehouse Pulled Pork (see p.29), chopped crispy bacon, slices of grilled veg, thinly sliced steak, chopped Brisket Burnt Ends (see p.74), sliced provolone cheese or chopped sun-dried tomatoes, or whatever else you fancy

METHOD

(1) Place 7 rashers of bacon vertically, side by side, on a chopping board. Interlace the remaining 7 bacon rashers horizontally to make a square lattice or 'bacon weave'. (See the photographs, p.116.)

(2) Spread the sausage meat in a 1cm-thick even layer over the top of the bacon weave, leaving a 2.5cm border top and bottom.

(3) Sprinkle the rub over the sausage meat until evenly coated.

(4) Top the sausage meat and rub with a layer of whatever filling you fancy – we've gone for 2 large handfuls of grated mozzarella.

(5) Carefully and tightly roll the bacon weave, encasing the filling, into a cylinder shape with the join underneath.

(6) Dust the outside of the bacon roll with more rub.

(7) Set up your BBQ to cook indirectly (see p.19) at a medium heat, around 150°C.

(8) Put the fatty on the BBQ and cook for around 1 hour or until the bacon is crisp and the internal temperature hits 75°C. Serve cut into thick slices.

BACON & CHIPOLATA BOMB

Here's a twist on the standard fatty recipe (opposite). It makes a great side dish for chicken or for Christmas day turkey (see p.122). The bacon weave is as before, but in place of the sausage meat, this version uses sage-and-onion stuffing with chipolatas as the filling.

FEEDS 2 AS A MAIN, OR 6 AS A SIDE

INGREDIENTS

14 thick streaky bacon rashers

6 chipolata sausages

For the stuffing

100g butter

2 tbsp olive oil

2 large onions, chopped

200g fresh breadcrumbs
(about ½ white loaf)

2 tbsp chopped fresh sage

salt and freshly ground
black pepper

METHOD

① To make the stuffing, heat the butter and oil in a saucepan over a medium heat. Add the onions and cook, stirring, for 5 minutes until softened. Stir in the breadcrumbs and sage, season, then leave to cool.

② To assemble the bomb, place 7 rashers of bacon vertically, side by side, on a chopping board. Interlace the remaining 7 bacon rashers horizontally to make a square lattice or 'bacon weave' (See top row of photographs, p.116.)

③ Spoon half the stuffing mixture widthways across the middle of the lattice; lay the chipolatas on top.

④ Spoon the rest of the stuffing mixture on top of the chipolatas in an even layer.

⑤ Carefully and tightly roll the bacon weave, encasing the filling, into a cylinder shape with the join underneath.

⑥ Set up your BBQ to cook indirectly (see p.19) at a medium heat, around 150°C.

⑦ Place the bomb in a roasting tin, seam-side down, and cook on the BBQ for 30 minutes or until firm and it holds its shape.

⑧ Remove the bomb from the tray and place directly on the grill rack for a further 30 minutes or until the bacon is crisp and the internal temperature hits 75°C. Serve cut into thick slices.

DJ★BBQ

SLOW & LOW
with Southern Soul
EST · 2012

THIS FOOD-TUBE CELEBRITY COOKBOOK AUTHOR AND
KICK-ASS PITMASTER ALSO KNOWS HOW TO GET
1,500 PEOPLE UP AND DANCING TO JOHN FARNHAM'S
'YOU'RE THE VOICE'. ABSOLUTE LEGEND.

DJ BBQ'S

★ FLANK STEAK ★

'Flank steak is my favourite cut of beef. My father would always grill a couple and serve 'em with a baked potato and salad. Classic American homely food. This recipe will rock your taste buds harder than something that rocks really hard. What? Sorry, been grilling a lot of burgers and smoking a lot of meat this summer.' - DJ BBQ

THIS MARINADE CAN HANDLE ABOUT 1KG OF FLANK. I LIKE COOKING FOR LOTS OF PEOPLE.

MARINADE INGREDIENTS

½ cup chopped garlic

250ml olive oil

60ml red wine vinegar

60ml lime juice (you can even use a microplane to zest some of the skin into the marinade)

1 tbsp soy sauce

1 chilli, chopped (get rid of the seeds if you want to dial down the heat)

1 tbsp freshly ground black pepper

1 pinch mustard powder

1 tsp ground cumin

half a bunch of coriander - chopped... use the stems and leaves, but save some of the leaves for decorating

METHOD

① Combine the marinade ingredients and throw this and 1kg flanks into a ziplock bag. Put it in the fridge. Do this the night before or the morning of the cookout - the vinegar will help tenderize the meat.

② The good thing about a flank steak is the muscle usually goes fatter towards the middle, so you can cook it for those that like well-done (the ends) to medium-rare (the middle) all in one steak. The ends are my favourite - they get all that marinade.

③ Set up your grill for two-zone cooking (see p.19). Before you grill, take the steak out of the fridge for 30 to 60 minutes. You want that muscle at room temperature. Pull the flank steak out of the marinade and let the excess oils drip off (to avoid flare-ups).

④ Hit it hot for 1-2 minutes a side to sear. You want grill marks. If you get flare-ups, move the steak to the indirect side for a bit. I grill my flank about 3-5 minutes a side depending on the cut and the heat. You need to poke it to see where it's at. It's done when it's done.

⑤ Rest it for half the time you cooked it. Slice against the grain and serve. Really good with tortillas and a pico de gallo salsa. Enjoy.

@DJ_BBQ

#djbbq

SANTA MARIA-STYLE TRI-TIP WITH CHIMICHURRI

Back in early 19th-century cowboy times, local Californian ranchers gathered to feast on large cuts of beef cooked over a fire. Their techniques have evolved into the regional speciality Santa Maria-style BBQ.

Santa Maria-style tri-tip is traditionally barbecued over red-oak logs on an adjustable grill. The sweet smoke gives the beef a distinctive flavour and unrivalled bark. If you can't find tri-tip, try large cuts of sirloin, fillet, picanha, or rump heart. Aim for the same internal temperatures, increasing the cooking time as necessary.

Californians serve tri-tip with pinto beans or a salsa. We like it on bread rolls with some punchy chimichurri.

FEEDS 4

INGREDIENTS

500g-1kg tri-tip (sometimes sold as rump-tail) or sirloin, fillet, picanha or rump heart

Beef Rub (see p.203)

The rest

Chimichurri (see p.195)

4 Tom Herbert's Buns (see p.168) (optional)

METHOD

① An hour before you plan to cook, season the beef all over with the rub. Leave it to come to room temperature.

② Set up your BBQ for two-zone cooking (see p.19) - the hotter, direct side at a high heat, around 220°C. Add your choice of smoking wood to the coals - we like to use oak, hickory and beech with beef.

③ Sear the beef by placing it on the hotter, direct side of the BBQ for 3-4 minutes per side. Don't be afraid of a little darkness - it's all good flavour.

④ Adjust the grill height or temperature, or move the beef to the cooler, indirect side of the grill, about 150°C. Cook for a further 10-15 minutes, turning occasionally, until the internal temperature hits 50°C for rare or 65°C for medium-well done. We like to cook to around 57°C.

⑤ Remove the beef from the BBQ, cover loosely with foil and leave it to rest for 10 minutes. Just before serving, slice the beef across the grain and serve on a board with the chimichurri on the side, or in buns with a good spoonful of the chimichurri on top of the meat.

BOURBON-BRINED TURKEY

Every day is a BBQ day and Christmas Day is no exception. This recipe takes the often bland, dry, generic turkey and pumps it up a few notches to a moist, crisp-skinned, subtly smoky bird of beauty. Brining increases the succulence and flavour of the turkey, helping the bird to retain moisture during cooking and preventing it drying out.

FEEDS 12

INGREDIENTS

6kg turkey, giblets removed

1 orange, halved

1 rosemary sprig

1-2 thyme sprigs

12 streaky bacon rashers

100g butter, melted, for brushing

For the bourbon brine

250g sea salt, preferably Maldon

250g light soft brown sugar
or 250ml maple syrup

250ml bourbon

about 15 whole black peppercorns

2 cloves

wide strips of zest from 2 lemons

a few bay leaves

METHOD

① To make the bourbon brine, heat 6 litres water in a large saucepan and stir in the salt and sugar or maple syrup until dissolved. Add the rest of the brine ingredients and leave to cool.

② Pat the turkey dry with kitchen paper and place it breast-side down in a cool box or large container with a lid. Pour the brine mixture over the turkey until it is completely submerged. Cover with a lid and refrigerate for 24 hours, turning it over halfway.

Alternatively, store the container in a cold garage or shed for 24 hours with frozen bottles of water packed around the turkey to keep it cool. Make sure you replace the frozen bottles every few hours.

③ Remove the turkey from the brine bath and pat dry with kitchen paper. Discard the brine.

④ Set up your BBQ to cook indirectly (see p.19) at a medium heat, around 160°C. Add your choice of smoking wood to the coals - we like to use pecan or fruit wood such as cherry or apple with poultry.

⑤ Put the 2 orange halves and the herbs in the turkey cavity; there is no need to season the bird. Arrange the bacon over the breast of the turkey. If you want to get fancy, you can make your turkey a bacon-weave jacket (see p.114). Make it feel special.

⑥ Put the turkey, breast-side up, on the BBQ and cook for 1 hour. Remove the bacon when crispy and brown. At this point every screaming ounce of your body will want to eat the bacon — this is normal, but you must resist.

⑦ Brush the turkey with melted butter (you could squeeze over some chargrilled orange, too) and again every 30 minutes. Continue to cook the turkey until its internal temperature hits 70°C, covering the bird with foil if it starts to burn (especially the wings and the ends of the legs) — about 4 hours in total. The turkey is ready when the skin is golden and the juices run clear when a skewer is inserted into the thickest part of the thigh.

⑧ Leave the turkey to rest for 20 minutes before carving — don't cover it with foil or the skin will lose its crispness. Now you can eat the bacon, on the side!

Maximum Rockgrass

HAYSEED DIXIE ARE THE CLOSEST THING WE HAVE TO
A HOUSE BAND. THEY'RE PART OF THE FURNITURE AT
GRILLSTOCK NOW. (AND THEIR VERSION OF 'HIGHWAY
TO HELL' IS BETTER THAN AC/DC'S.)

HAYSEED DIXIE'S
★ EAST ★ CHILLI
TENNESSEE

FEEDS 8

INGREDIENTS

680g minced beef

225g minced pork

½ bulb garlic, finely chopped
(around 5 large cloves)

500ml passata

1 tsp ground cumin

1 tsp ground coriander

1 tbsp cayenne pepper

1 tbsp hot smoked paprika

1 tbsp fennel seeds

1 tbsp hot chilli powder

1 tsp dried thyme

1 tbsp dried oregano

2 Scotch Bonnet chillies, seeded
and diced

1 Anaheim chilli, seeded and diced

2 poblano chillies, seeded and diced

2 green peppers, seeded and diced

1 red pepper, seeded and diced

1 tsp brown sugar

300g dried red kidney beans and
100g dried black beans,
soaked overnight

grated Monterey Jack cheese and
corn tortilla chips, to serve

METHOD

① Sear all the mince in a frying
pan over a reasonable heat until
it is browned thoroughly. Then
dump it in a Le Creuset-style big
cast iron dish along with the
garlic, passata, 250ml water,
spices, dried herbs, and chillies.

② Stir it up on the stove top and
bring it all to a nice bubbly sort
of gentle boil.

③ Then shove it in the BBQ,
cooking over indirect heat
for 2 hours at 150°C.

④ Take it out and stir it
every 20-30 minutes.

⑤ After 2 hours, add the green and
red peppers, brown sugar, and beans
to the chilli. You can use canned
beans, but it will be a whole lot
better if you use dried beans
that have been previously soaked
overnight, then vigorously boiled
for about 10 minutes and gently
boiled for around 30 minutes just
before you add them.

⑥ Let the whole concoction spend
1 additional hour in the BBQ.

⑦ Take the chilli out and serve
it up with grated Monterey Jack
cheese and corn tortilla chips.

@barleyscotch

www.hayseed-dixie.com

SALMON PLANK

Some good old-fashioned caveman cooking right here. Get a fire. Get a plank. Get a big fish. BOOM. Best salmon you ever ate. Cooking the fish on a plank works so well – it keeps the fish moist, and adds a huge hit of smoky flavour.

You can replicate the effect for a fish fillet using a smaller plank (soak it for four hours in water first) on the grill of your regular BBQ at medium heat.

FEEDS 4–5

INGREDIENTS

1kg side of salmon, skin on
(or a whole fish, filleted and butterflied, if you fancy)

3 lemons, halved

The rest

1 plank of oak, beech or other aromatic hard/fruit wood, about 1.2m long x 0.3m wide, dampened

drill, with 5mm drill bit

8 pieces of dowelling, about 5mm diameter x 4cm long, sharpened to a point at one end, and soaked

METHOD

① Lay the side of salmon on your plank of wood and sketch a rough outline around it with a pencil then remove the fish.

② Using the 5mm drill bit, drill 4 holes into the plank down one side of the drawn outline of the fish, roughly 2cm from the edge.

Repeat on the other side, making sure the holes on each side are directly opposite one another.

③ Place the salmon back on the plank, skin-side down, and secure it to the plank by carefully pressing the dowelling pegs through the fish into the holes.

④ We're cooking the fish next to a log fire so let the flames die down until you have lovely glowing logs and embers, rather than blazing heat.

⑤ Carefully place the plank vertically next to the fire, around 20cm away is good. Propping the plank up can be a little tricky, but we've found using a couple of large rocks as wedges works well.

This is a good recipe for the beach, as you can drive the plank into the sand to keep it upright.

⑥ Depending on the heat of the fire, the salmon should be hot smoked to perfection in around 1 hour. You can squeeze a little lemon juice over the fish if it looks like it is cooking too quickly. At the same time sear the remaining lemon halves on a grill rack over the fire until blackened in places, about 3 minutes.

⑦ When the salmon is ready, carefully carry the plank over to your table and arrange the lemon around the fish. Let everyone tuck in, squeezing the lemon over the fish, if they like.

MOINK BALLS

One of our favourite Chef's Choice dishes served up at the judges' table was a two-foot-high pyramid of moink balls by the From the Sauce competition BBQ team. A real showstopper!

Moink Balls are the 'moo' from a cow and the 'oink' from a pig: bacon-wrapped beef meatballs. On a stick. Smoked. KABOOM!

FEEDS 6 AS A MAIN, OR 12 AS A SIDE

INGREDIENTS

24 meatballs (shop-bought are fine, or, to make your own, see below)

24 smoked streaky bacon rashers

24 toothpicks

your favourite BBQ rub

Backyard BBQ Sauce (see p.194)

For the meatballs

1.5kg minced beef (20% fat)

2 eggs, lightly beaten

2 tbsp Worcestershire sauce

100g fresh breadcrumbs

1½ tsp sea salt, preferably Maldon

1 tbsp dried oregano

1½ tsp garlic powder

1½ tsp freshly ground black pepper

feel free to add any other spices you fancy - a shot of Grillstock House Rub (see p.202) is good

METHOD

① To make the meatballs, put all the ingredients in a large bowl and mix together by hand. Form the mince mixture into 24 meatballs, each about the size of a golf ball.

② Wrap a rasher of bacon around each meatball and secure with a toothpick, leaving one end of the pick sticking out further than the other - this will make the balls easier to eat.

Alternatively, instead of using cocktail sticks, you can load 3-4 moink balls onto a bamboo skewer. (Soak the bamboo skewers in water for 30 minutes first to stop them burning.)

③ Dust the moinks all over with your favourite rub.

④ Set up your BBQ to cook indirectly (see p.19) at a low heat, around 120°C.

⑤ Put the moinks on the BBQ and cook for 45 minutes or until the bacon turns crispy and the internal temperature hits just above 70°C.

⑥ At this point brush each moink ball all over with BBQ sauce and continue to cook, turning the balls occasionally until the saucy coating has caramelized.

REVEREND PEYTON'S BIG DAMN BAND IS THE REAL DEAL – BREEZY ON THE WASHBOARD AND REV PEYTON ON VARIOUS INCREDIBLE GUITARS. WE LOVE THEM.

REVEREND PEYTON'S
BACON-WRAPPED GOUDA-STUFFED
BBQ PRAWNS

FEEDS 3-4

INGREDIENTS

450-680g raw, shelled jumbo prawns, deveined

1 block of smoked Gouda

thick-cut streaky bacon rashers

soy sauce, or your favourite BBQ sauce, for brushing

METHOD

① Preheat a BBQ to medium temperature, around 160°C, and spray the grill with nonstick cooking spray. Butterfly the prawns – careful not to separate the two halves.

② Cut thin strips of Gouda and place one strip in the centre cut of each prawn.

③ Close the prawns around the cheese and wrap tightly from top to bottom with bacon. Brush some skewers with a little bit of soy sauce or your favourite BBQ sauce.

④ Skewer the wrapped prawns and BBQ on each side for 5 minutes or until the bacon is slightly crispy and the prawns are completely cooked through.

@bigdamnband
#bigdamnband
www.bigdamnband.com

PIT-BRAISED PULLED LAMB SHOULDER

In the smoky world of BBQ, when we talk about smoking a shoulder or two, pork gets all the glory. Probably because we're all looking at what the Americans are doing and – frankly – they're not all that into lamb.

Yep, we all know pulled pork is great, but pit-smoked and pulled lamb shoulder is off the chart. Another level. Watch and learn, America, you're missing a treat...

FEEDS 4-6

INGREDIENTS

2kg bone-in lamb shoulder

sea salt, preferably Maldon

freshly ground black pepper

Beef Rub (see p.203) (optional)

4-6 Tom Herbert's Buns (see p.168), split and lightly toasted

For the fresh mint sauce

75ml Jalapeño Vinegar (see p.200)

2 tbsp sugar

1 large bunch of torn mint leaves

METHOD

① Generously season the lamb all over with salt and pepper. (You could use beef rub, but avoid anything containing sugar or paprika as lamb is sweet enough.)

② Set up your BBQ to cook indirectly (see p.19) at a low heat, around 110°C. We're not fans of cooking lamb with too much smoke, so we advise to steer away from smoking woods. The lumpwood will give sufficient smoky flavour, but if you're a total smoke-head, go ahead and add some wood chunks.

③ Put the lamb on the BBQ and cook for 4-6 hours until the internal temperature hits 92°C. We're looking for a lovely chewy, golden bark for that perfect pulling point.

④ Transfer the lamb to a large tray, cover loosely with foil and leave to rest for 30 minutes while you make the fresh mint sauce.

⑤ To make the mint sauce, pour the vinegar into a bowl. Add the sugar, stir until it dissolves, then add the torn mint leaves. Stir until everything is mixed together and then set aside until ready to serve.

⑥ Pull the lamb away from the bone in hunks and then tease the strands apart with your fingers, throwing away any bits of bone and large pieces of fat. Make sure the deliciously seasoned bark is distributed evenly throughout so everyone gets a taste.

⑦ Pile the pulled lamb into a freshly toasted bun and douse with the mint sauce. The heat and the tang of the sauce work really well with the sweet, fatty lamb.

JACOB'S LADDER
BEEF RIB

Big, meaty hunks of succulent, smoky beef on the end of comedy dinosaur-size bones that wouldn't look out of place in *The Flintstones*... what's not to like? These are meaty lollipops at their very best.

This recipe relies on wrapping the ribs in a foil parcel after smoking to keep the moisture locked in and to render down the fat and connective tissue. If you prefer, you can pit-braise the ribs by placing them in a foil tray with beer, cider, wine or stock. Make sure the ribs are only half-submerged in your liquid of choice.

FEEDS 4

INGREDIENTS

about 2 Jacob's Ladder (short rib) beef racks, aim for 2-3 ribs per person

Beef Rub (see p.203)

100ml beer, cider, wine or stock

sea salt, preferably Maldon

Damn Fast Awesome Pickles (see p.178), to serve

METHOD

① First, remove the tough outer membrane from the ribs (see box, p.52). Trim off any excess fat or scraggy bits of meat to give two clean, neat racks.

② Liberally season the ribs all over with the rub. Leave them to stand for about 1 hour to come up to room temperature.

③ Set up your BBQ for smoking (see p.19), around 110°C. Add your choice of smoking wood to the coals - we like to use hickory and oak with beef. And avoid any woods that add a sweet flavour.

④ Put the ribs on the BBQ, bone-side down, and smoke for 3-4 hours until the meat has pulled back slightly to expose the end of the bone. The internal temperature should hit around 65°C.

⑤ Remove the rib racks from the BBQ and place each one on a large sheet of foil. Fold the edges of the foil over and crimp up the sides to make a pocket. Add the beer or other cooking liquid. Crimp the open end of each parcel to seal. (Double the foil if you're worried the bones will poke through.)

⑥ Return the ribs to the BBQ for another 2 hours. By then the meat will have drawn further up the bone and be incredibly tender and succulent. Give the meat a gentle tug, it should come away easily from the bone. The internal temperature should hit around 88°C at this point.

⑦ Remove the ribs from the BBQ and leave them to rest for 30 minutes in their foil parcels. Take the ribs out of the parcels and sprinkle with salt before slicing into individual bones to serve with pickles on the side.

IF YOU LIKE, YOU CAN FLASH THE RIBS ON A HOT GRILL OVER A DIRECT HEAT, A FEW MINUTES ON EACH SIDE, TO REVIVE THE CRUST.

EZ'S FISH TACOS

Fish tacos are an epic summer BBQ recipe – really simple and packed with freshness. Ez is Ben's wife and her tacos are inspired by a mix of Californian and Mexican flavours. The fruit salsa is a killer (experiment by adding your own mix of fruity goodness) – it goes with just about anything, but is best wrapped up with fresh fish, beer, and sunshine.

FEEDS 4–6

INGREDIENTS

2 heaped tbsp plain flour

½ tsp sea salt

½ tsp freshly ground black pepper

1 tsp cayenne pepper

1 tsp chilli powder

1 tsp dried chilli flakes

850g boneless, skinless cod loins or similar white meaty fish (or you could use salmon), patted dry and cut into bite-sized chunks

vegetable oil, for coating and cooking

12 soft mini flour tortillas

150g white cabbage, shredded

wedges of lime and/or a dash of Cholula Mexican hot sauce, to serve

For the fruit salsa

¼ honeydew melon, deseeded, skin removed and cubed

2 avocadoes, peeled, stone removed and cubed

2 kiwi fruits, peeled and cubed

100g blueberries

¼ pineapple, skin removed, cored and cubed

1 red chilli, deseeded and finely chopped

juice of ½ lime or more, to taste

1 handful of freshly chopped coriander leaves, about 2 tbsp

METHOD

① Set up your BBQ to cook directly (see p.18) at a medium heat, around 180°C.

② To make the fruit salsa, put all the ingredients in a bowl and mix gently but thoroughly. Taste and add more chilli, juice and/or coriander, if you like. Leave to one side.

(You could use other fruits, such as grapes or mango, or different types of melon. Mix it up!)

③ Mix together the flour, salt and spices on a large plate until combined. Roll the fish pieces in the spiced flour mixture until lightly coated all over, then shake off any excess.

④ Pour enough oil into a baking tray to coat the base and add the spiced flour-coated fish pieces. Shuffle them around gently so they get a bit of oil on each side, then spread out the fish chunks in the tray, so they have space in between.

⑤ Place a large cast iron skillet directly onto the hot coals of the BBQ and splash in some oil. Add the fish and cook for 5 minutes, turning once, or until very slightly crisp on the outside but still juicy in the middle – you don't want the fish to dry out! You may also find it easier to cook the fish in batches.

⑥ Warm the tortillas in a dry griddle pan. Fold the warm tacos in half ready for filling and line them up in a dish.

⑦ To assemble, put a pile of shredded cabbage on each tortilla, then top with the fish and a nice heap of salsa. Finish off with a squeeze of lime and/or a big dash of hot sauce. Wrap and eat.

SEARED SMOKED LEG OF LAMB

Who doesn't love a combo of a charred, sticky bark and slow-cooked, succulent meat? The trick is to get a good two-zone fire in your grill. Hot sear the lamb in one zone, then move it over to cook through.

FEEDS 8–10

INGREDIENTS

4kg bone-in leg of lamb

Taters (see p.175), to serve

Herb wet rub

4–5 anchovies in oil, drained

1 garlic clove, peeled

2 tbsp Dijon mustard

juice of 1 lemon

1 large bunch of rosemary leaves

2 tbsp olive oil

10g sea salt, preferably Maldon

freshly ground black pepper

METHOD

① To make the rub, put the anchovies, garlic, mustard, lemon juice, rosemary, oil and salt in a food processor. Season with pepper and blitz to a rough paste, adding more oil if is too thick. Alternatively, chop the anchovies and rosemary by hand and combine with the rest of the ingredients.

② Make deep, diagonal slashes along the top of the lamb and put it in a roasting tin. Massage half the herb wet rub liberally all over the lamb, getting it into all the cuts. Leave the lamb for 1 hour or so to come up to room temperature.

③ Set up your BBQ for two-zone cooking (see p.19), the hotter, direct side at a medium heat, around 160°C.

④ Put the lamb on the hot side of the BBQ and cook for 15 minutes, turning it every 2-3 minutes until seared and browned all over.

⑤ Now move the lamb over to the cooler, indirect side of the BBQ to cook through. At this point decide if you're going to roast the lamb hot 'n' fast or cook it low 'n' slow. For hot-'n'-fast action, keep the BBQ temperature at around 160°C and cook the lamb with the lid on for a further 45 minutes, or until the internal temperature hits 65°C, when the lamb will be pink and juicy.

For low 'n' slow, put the lid on and clamp down the vents at the bottom of the BBQ until the temperature stabilizes at around 120°C. Cook the lamb until the internal temperature hits around 90°C (about 5 hours), by which point it will shred beautifully.

⑥ Remove the lamb from the BBQ. Cover loosely with foil and leave to rest for 30 minutes. Slice or pull the lamb and serve with the remaining herb wet rub drizzled over the top, and golden taters by the side.

MOTLEY-QUE

CREW

THE MOTLEY-QUE CREW BBQ TEAM IS WELL KNOWN ON THE COMPETITION CIRCUIT.
WE HUNG OUT WITH THEM IN KANSAS AND LOVED THE SOUND OF THIS RECIPE.

MOTLEY-QUE CREW'S
★ TIGER STEAK ★
MOTLEY-QUE'D

FEEDS 9

INGREDIENTS

2 large Yukon Gold potatoes

spice mixture: sea salt, freshly ground black pepper and garlic powder, to taste

2-3 prime fillet steaks, about 2.5cm thick with nice marbling

sour cream, for dolloping

Tiger sauce, for drizzling

METHOD

Potato croustade

Peel and grate the potatoes, then season with some of the spice mixture, to taste.

Flatten out the potato mixture to a thickness of around 1cm.

Use a 6cm-diameter cookie cutter to cut the potato into 9 croustades.

Steak

Season the steaks with some spice mixture.

Cooking

Griddle the potato croustades until crispy and browned, then reserve.

Grill the steaks over hot charcoal (we like the brand Kingsford) to a perfect medium-rare (see p.148), then let it rest for 5-10 minutes before cutting into 4cm squares.

Assembly

1. Potato croustade

2. Dollop of sour cream

3. Top with steak

4. Drizzle of Tiger sauce

STEAK WITH PEPPERCORN SAUCE

Grilling up a thick rib-eye and going to the trouble of cooking a delicious peppercorn sauce on the side shows someone you care. This is the go-to 'birthday dinner' in our house. Even for the cat.

FEEDS 4

INGREDIENTS

oil, for brushing the grill

4 rib-eye steaks, cut to your chosen thickness

sea salt, preferably Maldon

freshly ground black pepper

For the peppercorn sauce

25g butter

½ onion, finely chopped

3-4 mushrooms, sliced (optional)

1 tbsp bourbon

2 tbsp coarsely ground pink and black peppercorns

150ml Worcestershire sauce

150ml double cream

METHOD

① Set up your BBQ to cook directly (see p.18) at a high heat, around 220°C. Screaming hot is good. Make sure the grill bars are clean and well oiled.

② Season the steaks with salt and pepper and let them come up to room temperature.

③ Gently lay the steaks down on the BBQ and cook for 2-3 minutes on each side, continuing to flip and check the steaks until cooked to your liking.

Use the temperatures given on page 148 as a guide to doneness. Bear in mind that the steak will continue to cook for a minute or so even when it's taken off the grill.

④ Remove the steaks from the BBQ. Cover loosely with foil and leave to rest for 10 minutes or so while you make the peppercorn sauce.

⑤ Melt the butter in a saucepan and sauté the onion and mushrooms, if using, until softened and starting to brown.

⑥ Carefully pour in the bourbon and deglaze the pan, stirring to loosen and dissolve any bits stuck to the bottom.

⑦ Add the pepper, Worcestershire sauce and double cream and simmer for 5-10 minutes, stirring often, until the sauce has reduced and thickened. Check for potency and add more pepper or double cream, as required.

⑧ Finally, pour any juices from the rested steak into the sauce. Serve the steaks with the sauce spooned on top or by the side.

HOW TO COOK THE PERFECT STEAK

Whole books have been written on how to cook a perfect steak. Really, though, it boils down to just a small handful of factors, the rest is fluff. Here are our golden rules for grilling a steak to perfection. Learn them well.

• Pay for good-quality meat. Choose a well-marbled, dry-aged cut — rib-eye and sirloin are our top two. If you're on a budget, buy a smaller piece of better-quality meat.

• Ask your butcher to cut your steaks to your chosen thickness. You want a minimum 2.5cm thickness. And anything up to 5cm is even better. Thicker cuts allow you to build up a good sear on the outside without overcooking the middle. Thin steaks cook too quickly.

• Allow your steaks to come up to room temperature before you cook them.

• Invest in an instant-read thermometer to cook to your preferred exact level of doneness. An internal temp of 54°C gives you rare; 57°C for how we do it at Grillstock; 62°C for medium; and 68°C or higher for well done. Allow for the fact that the steaks will keep on cooking, rising by a few more degrees even after you take them off the grill. So, if you want your steak medium, take it off the grill at 58-60°C. (Precisely how much it rises will depend on the size of the steak, as well as the ambient temperature.)

• Season with nothing more than Maldon sea salt and freshly ground black pepper — a sprinkling before you cook and a second hit just before you eat.

• Cook your steaks over very hot, glowing coals, not flames. Despite the adverts for cheap burgers, 'flame-grilled' is not cool.

• Try to cook your steak with your BBQ lid down — this helps reduce flare-ups from dripping fat.

• Once the steak hits the grill don't poke or squeeze it down. Allow a sear to build evenly.

• Flip your steaks three times, so each surface gets two sessions in the direct heat. The frequency of the flipping depends on how thick your steaks are and how hot your fire is.

• Rest your steaks for a minimum 10 minutes under loosely tented foil, allowing all the juices to redistribute and the meat to relax before you eat.

> NOT MUCH BEATS A PERFECTLY COOKED STEAK, SO KEEP IT SIMPLE. BUY GOOD MEAT AND TREAT IT WELL.

BRISTOL CHEESESTEAK SANDWICH

Philly cheesesteak sandwiches are up there with the best kind of sandwich: thin steak, gooey melted cheese and a soft bread roll. Simple, quick and satisfying food on the go. It is claimed the original Philly cheesesteak was invented back in the 1930s by Pat and Harry Olivieri – a couple of hot-dog vendors who decided to try something different in Philadelphia. Of course, this might be utter baloney, but we like a good story behind our food.

Over in America every diner has a particular version of this sandwich. Well, we have our own version, too, and we call it the Bristol cheesesteak... mainly because we came up with it in Bristol.

FEEDS 4

INGREDIENTS

2 bavette steaks or similar, about 200g each

Beef Rub (see p.203)

glug of olive oil

1 onion, finely chopped

1 yellow pepper, deseeded and cut into small dice

8 American-style cheese slices

200g Cheddar cheese, grated

The rest

4 large hot dog rolls, split

Hot BBQ Sauce (see p.194) or Ketchup (see p.196)

Damn Fast Awesome Pickles (see p.178)

METHOD

① An hour before you plan to start cooking, sprinkle the steaks all over with the rub. Leave the steaks to come up to room temperature.

② Set up your BBQ to cook directly (see p.18) at a high heat, around 250°C.

③ Flash grill the steaks for a minute or two on each side, turning them a couple of times, until the internal temperature hits around 54°C for rare. Leave the steaks to rest and cool, then cut into very thin slices. (If you have time, stick the cooked, cooled steaks in the fridge and

While playing around with this recipe, we invented a brisket version. Instead of using the bavette, take your leftover Smokehouse Brisket (see p.70) from the fridge and slice as thinly as possible – a deli-slicer is ideal if you have access to one. Serve as above.

slice when chilled right down – it'll be easier to cut them thinly.)

④ Heat a good glug of olive oil in a large cast iron skillet on the hob over a medium-high heat. Add the onion and cook until it starts to brown, stirring often. Add the yellow pepper and cook for a further 2 minutes until softened.

⑤ Gently fold in the sliced steak and cook until heated through.

⑥ Lay the cheese slices over the meat and veg in the pan. Sprinkle over the Cheddar, cover the pan with a lid and heat through for 30 seconds or until the cheese starts to melt.

⑦ Divide the filling between the hot dog rolls, dump in some hot BBQ sauce and pickles and eat, resisting the urge to stuff it all in at once. Remember to breathe.

THE ELVIS

Inspired by our deep-rooted love for all things Elvis, this toasted sandwich celebrates what we now claim as FACT to be the last meal the King ever ate.

We're not really sure who came up with this recipe. Jon thought it was Dan, Dan says it was Jon. Might even have been Jon's brother Bob, come to think of it.

It doesn't really matter all that much.

It's been sold as a bit of fun at our St Nick's take-out place for the last few years – a secret option not listed on the menu. You have to know it's there and ask for it by name.

You can cook it in a pie iron on the BBQ or in the embers of a fire, in a toasted-sandwich maker, or in a non-stick frying pan or on a griddle. Uh huh huh.

FEEDS 1

INGREDIENTS

2 slices of white bread

butter, for spreading

1 tbsp peanut butter

2 cooked streaky bacon rashers

1 ripe banana, sliced

75g Smokehouse Pulled Pork (see p.29)

1 green chilli, deseeded and sliced into rounds

1 tbsp maple syrup

METHOD

① Spread one side of each slice of bread thickly with butter.

② Spread the peanut butter on the non-buttered side of one slice.

③ Lay the cooked bacon on the peanut butter.

④ Top the bacon with the banana.

⑤ Next, evenly distribute the pulled pork on top.

⑥ Scatter the chilli over.

⑦ Drizzle with maple syrup.

⑧ Place the non-buttered side of the second slice of bread on top of the filling. You should now have a pretty epic-looking sandwich with butter smeared on the outside.

⑨ Put the Elvis in a pie iron or cast iron frying pan directly on the hot coals (or on a hob over a medium heat). When the bread is golden, carefully flip it over and cook the other side until browned, about 5 minutes on each side.

⑩ Serve, telling your fellow diners that this is the last sandwich Elvis ever ate. FACT.

Thank yuh very much.

PIE IRONS ARE A VERY UNDERRATED BIT OF KIT. THEY'RE LIKE A TOASTIE MAKER FOR YOUR BBQ OR FIRE PIT.

BURGERS

HOW TO MAKE A GREAT BURGER

When we opened our first Smokehouse, we spent three months perfecting our house burger patty. Admittedly, it was a fun three month's 'work' – and it was also very worthwhile, as our burger went on to win Best Burger in both Bristol's and Bath's Good Food Awards.

There are four main things to consider in a great burger:

1. The choice of your meat cuts (for flavour/meat-to-fat ratio/ texture and so on)

2. How fine or coarse you grind your meat

3. The seasoning

4. The size and shape of your patty formation

In our burgers we like to use cuts such as skirt, flank, chuck, brisket and neck – these offer great flavour and you can mix them up to get the right fat content. Aim for 80 percent meat and 20 percent fat. Or 30 percent fat if you like the juice running right up to your elbows, rather than stopping at your wrists.

Grinding your own meat is a wonderful thing to do – it gives you ultimate control over all the variables. Plus, you'll be sure that only good meat is going in. You don't need fancy kit really. You can pick up a cast iron, hand-cranked mincing machine for as little as a tenner on the Internet. Or, you can get an attachment that fits onto your existing food mixer.

Chill the beef right down in the fridge, chop into small chunks and grind it twice on a medium grind plate – around 5mm.

Do not add seasoning as you grind. Salt starts to break down the proteins in meat and begins to bind the meat together. You know how it feels – when you bite into a patty that has the texture of a sausage, rather than a lovely fall-apart, tender burger? That.

Once you've done your grinding, roll the meat into a ball and press down into a rough circle around 1cm thick. Don't press too hard or handle the meat too much. Loose patties are good.

GRILLSTOCK BURGER

Picasso said you need to know the rules before you can break them. He was probably referring to art rather than meat, but the sentiment stays the same. Before you go off getting all fancy with your burger toppings, make sure your base burger is absolutely dialled. It's the foundation for greater things to come.

Like we said in the intro to the book, it's usually the more basic burgers that win our annual competition. Do simple things extraordinarily well.

FEEDS 4

INGREDIENTS

500g minced beef, a mix of 50% neck and 50% brisket or skirt

Beef Rub (see p.203)

The rest

4 Tom Herbert's Buns (see p.168), split and lightly toasted

ketchup

shredded iceberg lettuce

sliced tomato

sliced red onion

Comeback Sauce (see p.200)

METHOD

① Form the minced beef into 4 equal-sized patties.

② Set up your BBQ to cook directly (see p.18) at a high heat, around 250°C. Add a solid handful of wood chunks, if you like.

③ Put the burgers on the BBQ, dust the tops with a pinch of beef rub and cook for 2-3 minutes on each side, dusting with more rub after turning. Ideally, close the lid on your BBQ as this will help prevent flare-ups.

④ Remove the burgers from the BBQ, cover loosely with foil and leave to rest for a few minutes, while you toast the buns.

⑤ Now build up each burger, from the ground up: bun, ketchup, Grillstock burger patty, lettuce, tomato, red onion, sauce and bun.

GRILLSTOCK BACON CHEESEBURGER

Once your friends are referring to your base burger (see opposite) as the best they ever ate, you're allowed to move on and start dropping a few extra toppings into the mix. This classic bacon cheeseburger takes some beating and really relies on having good bacon.

The Smokestack™ (below) is the best-selling burger in our restaurants and it treats people to your pulled pork, too. Don't eat the chilli burger on a first date.

FEEDS 4

INGREDIENTS

1kg minced beef, a mix of 50% neck and 50% brisket or skirt

Beef Rub (see p.203)

8 American-style cheese slices

The rest

4 Tom Herbert's Buns (see p.168), split and lightly toasted

ketchup

Damn Fast Awesome Pickles (p.178)

8-12 grilled thick streaky bacon rashers

Comeback Sauce (p.200)

METHOD

① Form the minced beef into 8 equal-sized patties.

② Set up your BBQ to cook directly (see p.18) at a high heat, around 250°C. Add a solid handful of wood chunks, if you like.

③ Next, cook the burgers in the same way as the Grillstock Burger (see step 3, opposite). Two minutes after you flip the burgers, place a cheese slice on top of each one and cook for a further minute.

④ Remove the burgers from the BBQ, cover loosely with foil and leave to rest for a few minutes, while you toast the buns.

⑤ Now build up each burger, from the ground up: bun, ketchup, pickle, burger with cheese, bacon rashers, burger with cheese, bacon rashers, sauce and bun.

GRILLSTOCK SMOKESTACK™ BURGER

Make this like the Grillstock Bacon Cheeseburger, but use a single cheeseburger and swap the bacon for 100g Smokehouse Pulled Pork (see p.29).

GRILLSTOCK CHILLI BURGER

Make this like the Grillstock Bacon Cheeseburger, but use a single cheeseburger with a good spoonful of Hillbilly Chilli (see p.78) and sour cream, if you fancy, instead of the bacon and sauce.

THE BEEFY BOYS

THE BEEFY BOYS WON BEST BURGER AT GRILLSTOCK IN 2014, THEN HEADED OFF TO COMPETE IN THE USA. NOW BACK IN THE UK, THEY HAVE THEIR OWN BURGER JOINT.

BEEFY BOYS'
★ BUTTY BACK BURGER ★

GRAND FINALE WINNER 'BEST BURGER' AT THE WORLD FOOD CHAMPIONSHIPS

MAKES 1 BURGER

INGREDIENTS

The patty

110g leftover smoked brisket

Butty Bach ale

favourite BBQ sauce

150g freshly ground, grass-fed, dry-aged rib beef with a 70:30 meat-to-fat ratio.

Secret Beefy Boys Burger Seasoning made from salt, *****, *****, ***** and ***** (or use a pinch or two of Grillstock Beef Rub, see p.203)

Red cabbage slaw

red cabbage, white cabbage, carrot, red onion, white wine vinegar, sugar, salt, mayo, yogurt

The rest

semi brioche bun

Swiss cheese slice

American cheese slice

lettuce

red onion

@thebeefyboys
www.thebeefyboys.com

METHOD

① Chop up the leftover brisket and gently heat it in a pan with a glug each of the Butty Bach ale and BBQ sauce. Reduce the liquid until you get a thick, meaty, paste-like sauce, with the brisket pulled apart into strands. Season and add more BBQ sauce or Butty to balance the consistency – not too runny. Set aside somewhere warm.

② Shred the slaw veg and mix with a dash of vinegar, sugar and salt. Leave for 30 minutes, then mix with the mayo and yogurt. Set aside.

③ Form the ground beef into a patty shape that's wide enough for the meat to hang out of the bun. Cover and leave to come up to room temperature. DO NOT SEASON! Slice and toast the brioche bun.

④ Cook the patty over a high heat. Either direct grill on the BBQ or, for diner-style, use a hot plate over the coals. Make an indent in the centre with your thumb to stop the patty balling up. Season the top and cook for 2–3 minutes, then flip and season again. Cook to your desired doneness. If it's squidgy it's rare; bouncy, it's medium; solid, it's well done. Add a slice each of the cheeses to the patty, then remove from the grill and assemble: bun, slaw, lettuce, onion, brisket mix, cheesy patty, bun.

LOCKJAW™

There are two kinds of burger in this world: the kind that you just pick up and wolf down, and the kind that commands respect, instils fear and demands an eating strategy.

The Lockjaw sits firmly in the latter camp. Our custom burger patties are the foundation of a smoky, juicy tower of awesomeness, layered up with not just hickory-smoked pulled pork, but also thick slices of pit-smoked brisket and a pile of Brisket Burnt Ends (see p.74), those glorious nuggets of BBQ gold.

Attempt this recipe when you're having a major cookout day. It's worth the effort.

SERVES 1

INGREDIENTS

1 Tom Herbert's Bun (see p.168), split and lightly toasted

Damn Fast Awesome Pickles (see p.178)

Smokehouse Pulled Pork (see p.29)

2 Grillstock Burger patties (see p.158), freshly cooked

2 American-style cheese slices

several slices of Smokehouse Brisket (see p.70)

a pile of Brisket Burnt Ends (see p.74)

Comeback Sauce (see p.200)

METHOD

You've done the hard work — you've made the component parts — so all you need here is some construction advice. From the ground up:

1. Lay out the bun base.

2. Layer on some pickles.

3. Add a small handful of pulled pork.

4. Place on top burger patty #1.

5. Top this burger with a cheese slice.

6. Add some brisket.

7. Layer on burger patty #2.

8. Top this burger with the second cheese slice.

9. Add some burnt ends.

10. Drizzle over some sauce.

11. Relax, the tower's still standing — finish it off with the bun top.

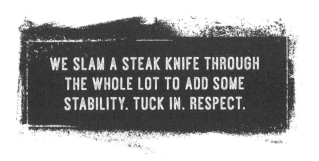

WE SLAM A STEAK KNIFE THROUGH THE WHOLE LOT TO ADD SOME STABILITY. TUCK IN. RESPECT.

★ FIXIN'S ★

TOM HERBERT'S BUNS

Tom is a fifth-generation baker working in the family business, Hobbs House Bakery, in South Gloucestershire.

He launched the bakery's 'Ultimate Burger Bap' onto the market at the Grillstock Festival several years ago and we've used it in our Smokehouses ever since. So often a great burger or sandwich is let down by a rubbish, cheap bread roll. You have to put in the effort to give your pulled pork roll the foundations it deserves. Do it. Invest in your meat's happiness.

MAKES 10

INGREDIENTS

500g strong white flour

1 tbsp caster sugar

25g lard or butter

10g salt

200ml tepid milk

5g dried yeast

100ml tepid water

1 egg, beaten

sesame seeds, to sprinkle over

METHOD

① Weigh the flour, sugar, lard and salt into a large bowl and add the milk. Mix the yeast with the tepid water, add it to the bowl and mix thoroughly into a dough. Turn the dough out onto a lightly floured surface and knead for 10 minutes until it is soft and elastic. Leave it to rise for 1 hour in a covered bowl left in a warm place.

② Divide the dough into 10 pieces and on a lightly floured surface roll into balls with your hands. Then using a rolling pin flatten into 10cm baps on a floured surface. Place on baking trays lined with baking paper and brush beaten egg over each bun. Cover loosely with cling film and leave them in a warm place for 30 minutes.

③ Brush with a second coat of beaten egg and sprinkle a pinch of sesame seeds onto each bun. Cover loosely with cling film and leave to rise for a final 30 minutes.

④ Meanwhile, preheat your oven to 200°C/fan 180°C/gas mark 6. Bake the buns until they are perfectly golden, about 10-15 minutes.

LOUISIANA DIRTY RICE

It's perfectly legit to cook this on your smoker or BBQ, or even in the embers of a log fire. You'll get pitmaster points from us for doing so. Frankly, though, this recipe does not call for much of a smoke flavour and it might be easier just cooked on a regular hob.

The method looks a little lengthy, but dirty rice is really pretty quick and easy to make. A big pot will go a long way and accompany your delicious pit-smoked meats perfectly.

The chicken livers give the dish its trademark flavour, but it's okay to leave them out if you prefer. We won't judge you. Feel free to add some bacon at the start, if you like.

FEEDS 8–10

INGREDIENTS

1 tbsp olive oil, for frying

500g sausage meat (or your favourite sausages squeezed out of their skins)

500g chicken livers, finely chopped

1 large onion, finely chopped

1 celery stick, finely chopped

1 green pepper, deseeded and diced

3 garlic cloves, minced

500g leftover Smokehouse Brisket (see p.70), chopped into small bits

500g white long-grain rice

about 1 litre chicken stock

2 tbsp Worcestershire sauce

2 tsp Grillstock House Rub (see p.202)

½ tsp cayenne pepper or chipotle powder

1 bunch of spring onions, chopped

20g parsley leaves, chopped

METHOD

① Heat the oil in a large cast iron pan over a medium heat. Add the sausage meat and chicken livers and fry for 5 minutes, stirring regularly to break up any clumps and lumps and until browned all over.

② Add the onion, celery, green pepper and garlic to the pan and cook for another 5 minutes, stirring often, until softened.

③ Add the smoked brisket, followed by the rice and let everything cook for a couple of minutes, stirring.

④ Pour in the stock and Worcestershire sauce, then add the rub and cayenne or chipotle. Bring to the boil, then reduce the heat to low, cover with a lid, and simmer for 20 minutes until the rice is cooked and the stock has been absorbed. (Add more hot water, if needed.)

⑤ Stir in the spring onions and parsley, reserving some to sprinkle over the rice at the end. Cover and leave to stand off the heat for 10 minutes.

⑥ Sprinkle with the rest of the parsley and serve.

JALAPEÑO BACON POPPERS

Dan, who runs our St. Nick's shack in Bristol, started serving these up once a week as a lunchtime special. They very quickly became a permanent fixture on the menu and it's easy to see why.

The heat of the jalapeño chilli is tamed by a rich, cream-cheese filling before being wrapped in a crisp, 'bacony' hug. Delicious.

MAKE MORE THAN YOU EXPECT TO EAT. ONCE YOU POP YOU JUST CAN'T STOP.

FEEDS 4

INGREDIENTS

20 jalapeño chilli peppers, halved lengthways and deseeded

250g cream cheese

10 streaky bacon rashers, cut in half crossways

METHOD

① Set up your BBQ to cook indirectly (see p.19) at a medium heat, around 160°C.

② Using a teaspoon, fill each jalapeño half almost to the brim with cream cheese.

③ Wrap a slice of bacon around each jalapeño to keep in the cream-cheese filling and secure with a cocktail stick, if needed.

④ Put the jalapeño poppers in a roasting tray on the BBQ and cook for around 20 minutes, turning occasionally, until the bacon is golden and crispy and the peppers have softened.

POTATO SALAD

We remember family BBQs when we were kids as some bangers and burgers served up with a big bowl of potato salad. It's a classic side to a BBQ and deserves to be there. Across the Atlantic people argue just as much about what makes a good potato salad as they do about the best way to smoke ribs. It's emotive.

Our base version sails close to what we grew up with, but we've seen some really interesting additions on our travels and we've shared those options with you, too.

FEEDS 6-8

INGREDIENTS

1kg waxy new potatoes, Charlotte is good, cut into 1cm cubes

200g mayonnaise

1 tbsp plain yogurt

1 tbsp French's yellow mustard

a pinch or two of Beef Rub (see p.203)

1 bunch of spring onions, finely chopped

6 cooked-until-crisp streaky bacon rashers, crumbled

METHOD

① Boil the potatoes for about 10 minutes until tender but not soft, then drain. Put the potatoes in a serving bowl and leave to cool.

② Add the rest of the ingredients to the bowl and mix gently until combined. Ideally, chill the potato salad for a couple of hours in the fridge before serving.

ADD GHERKIN & EGG

Try adding chopped gherkins and chopped hard-boiled eggs to the potato salad.

DRESS WITH VINAIGRETTE

Instead of the traditional mayo/yogurt dressing, try the following vinaigrette.

Ingredients

2 tbsp red or white wine vinegar

¼ tsp sea salt, preferably Maldon

2 tsp Dijon mustard

5 tbsp extra-virgin olive oil

freshly ground black pepper

Method

Mix together all the ingredients for the dressing in a bowl. Spoon it over the potato salad.

TRY A RANCH DRESSING

Another dressing to try is Ranch.

Ingredients

125ml plain yogurt or buttermilk

1 tbsp chopped dill

1 tsp onion powder

½ garlic clove, minced

1 tbsp lemon juice

a pinch each of sea salt and freshly ground black pepper

Method

Mix together all the ingredients for the dressing in a bowl. Spoon it over the potato salad.

TATERS

These BBQ roasted potatoes are dead easy to make... plus there's no washing up to do afterwards.

If you want to speed things up, par-boil the potatoes first, but make sure they're on the BBQ long enough to get some good crisp-and-tasty char marks.

FEEDS 4–6

INGREDIENTS

650g waxy new potatoes, such as Charlotte, halved if large

4–5 garlic cloves, left whole and unpeeled

2 rosemary sprigs

very generous glug of olive oil

sea salt (preferably Maldon) and freshly ground black pepper, or Grillstock House Rub (see p.202)

METHOD

1. Set up your BBQ to cook directly (see p.18) at a high heat, about 200°C.

2. Tear off a sheet of foil, about 1 metre long. Use the thickest foil you can for this – catering is best. Fold the foil in half, so you end up with a double-thick sheet around 50cm long. Fold the foil in half again and then crimp the two sides to make a pocket, leaving the top open.

3. Tip the potatoes, garlic, rosemary and a very generous glug of oil into the foil pocket. Season with salt and pepper or house rub. Crimp the open end to make a sealed parcel, then give everything a damn good shake.

4. Put the parcel on the BBQ and cook for 25–30 minutes, giving the bag a shake every 10 minutes until the potatoes are tender and charred in places.

5. To serve, carefully cut open the pocket and tip the entire contents into a bowl.

GRILLSTOCK MAC 'N' CHEESE

Everyone loves mac 'n' cheese. It makes a comforting side to pretty much any BBQ meat. We elevate it to a dish in its own right in the Smokehouses by topping it with a handful of freshly smoked pulled pork and a hit of BBQ sauce before serving. You could do the same with some crispy bacon or even leftover rib meat – anything porky works.

FEEDS 4

INGREDIENTS

1 tbsp olive oil

500g elbow macaroni

70g butter

70g plain flour

500ml whole milk, warmed

500g mature Cheddar cheese, grated

a squirt of French's yellow mustard

2 tsp Beef Rub (see p.203)

a good handful of crispy bacon pieces

Damn Fast Awesome Pickles (see p.178), to serve

METHOD

① Set up your BBQ to cook indirectly (see p.19) at a medium heat, around 160°C.

② Brush the inside of a heavy-duty baking dish or cast iron skillet with the oil.

③ Bring a large saucepan of salted water to the boil. Add the macaroni and cook until it is tender but still has a little bite left, about 8-10 minutes. Drain through a colander, then rinse the macaroni in cold water and set aside.

④ Melt the butter in a saucepan over a medium-low heat and sprinkle in the flour. Using a wooden spoon, beat well to make a roux or smooth paste, then turn the heat to low and cook the roux for a minute or two.

⑤ Pour a third of the warm milk into the pan, whisking continuously, until smooth and heated through. Gradually, whisk in the rest of the milk and cook for 3-4 minutes until the sauce is smooth and has thickened.

⑥ Take the pan off the heat, tip in the cheese, mustard and rub and stir until the cheese melts.

⑦ Mix the cheese sauce and macaroni together until combined, then tip into the oiled dish.

⑧ Put the dish on the BBQ and cook for 30 minutes or until the top is golden and bubbling.

⑨ Sprinkle the bacon over the mac 'n' cheese before serving, with pickles by the side.

DAMN FAST AWESOME PICKLES

We serve these pickles on every tray of food in the Grillstock Smokehouses. They're perfect for cutting through the rich, smoky, fatty BBQ meats, but they also make a great side to pretty much anything.

Once you've made the pickles, bottle them in sterilized jars (see below) and leave them for a couple of days in the fridge for the flavours to really come out. Although, if you can't wait that long, you could tuck in as soon as they've chilled down.

MAKES ABOUT 1KG (DRAINED WEIGHT)

INGREDIENTS

2 large cucumbers, cut into 3mm thick slices

1 onion, cut into 3mm thick slices

1 red pepper, deseeded and cut into 3mm thick slices

40g salt

For the pickling brine

500ml cider vinegar

250g caster sugar

1 tbsp yellow mustard seeds

½ tbsp coriander seeds

1 tbsp pink peppercorns

½ tsp turmeric

¼ tsp ground cloves

METHOD

① Put the sliced vegetables in a big bowl with the salt and toss until everything is coated in the salt. Put something heavy, such as a plate topped with a weight, directly on top of the veg. Leave the vegetables to sit for 3–4 hours until they release their liquid content.

② Tip the veg into a colander and rinse thoroughly under a cold running tap to remove the salt, then drain well and pat dry with kitchen paper.

③ To make the pickling brine, put the vinegar, sugar and spices in a saucepan with 400ml water. Bring to the boil over a medium heat, stirring until the sugar dissolves. As soon as the brine starts to boil, add the veg to the pan, return to the boil, then immediately take the pan off the heat.

④ Spoon the pickles into sterilized jars (see below) and top with tight-fitting lids. Leave the pickles to cool, then place in the fridge ideally for 2 days before eating. The pickles will keep unopened in the fridge for up to 6 weeks. Once opened eat within 1 week.

> STERILIZE YOUR JARS BY RUNNING THEM THROUGH THE DISHWASHER ON ITS HOTTEST SETTING. LEAVE THEM TO DRY COMPLETELY BEFORE FILLING. MAKE SURE YOU ALWAYS USE NEW LIDS IF YOU'RE REUSING JARS.

ONE-HOUR PICKLED ONIONS

Bish bash bosh. You can knock up these pickled onions in minutes and be eating them only an hour later.

They make a great side to any smoked meats or toss them into any sandwich you're making.

MAKES ABOUT 300G

INGREDIENTS

100g white sugar

1 large red or white onion, thinly sliced

60ml cider vinegar

2 tbsp black peppercorns

fresh herbs or spices of your choosing, such as thyme or oregano sprigs, coriander seeds, mustard seeds, jalapeño chilli peppers, or chilli flakes

METHOD

1. Pour 100ml hot water into a big bowl. Add the sugar and stir until it dissolves.

2. Add the rest of the ingredients, stir well and leave to stand for 1 hour before using. Or you can keep the pickled onions in the fridge in an airtight container or spoon them into a sterilized jar (see opposite) and store for up to 1 week.

BRAISED FENNEL

This dish is the perfect accompaniment to the porchetta on page 38.

FEEDS 8

INGREDIENTS

6 fennel bulbs, thinly sliced (preferably with a mandolin — mind your fingers)

500ml chicken stock, or enough to cover

a few thyme sprigs

2 tbsp fennel seeds

METHOD

1. Put the fennel in a saucepan and pour over enough chicken stock to cover.

2. Add the thyme and fennel seeds and bring almost to the boil. Reduce the heat and simmer gently, part-covered, for about 30 minutes or until the fennel is soft and tender.

MEXICAN GRILLED CORN

Most of us are pre-programmed to think we have to boil or steam corn before it goes anywhere near a grill, but there's really no need to. This classic Mexican street food is cooked and charred entirely on the BBQ, resulting in crunchy kernels with a buttery, creamy, spicy hit. A bit of sweet, a bit of heat and a kick of lime. A flavour sensation.

HUNT DOWN CORN IN ITS HUSK. YOU CAN USE THE LEAVES TO CREATE FANCY-LOOKING HANDLES TO MAKE THE CORN EASIER TO EAT.

FEEDS 8

INGREDIENTS

8 corn cobs, husk on

100g soft butter or mayonnaise

1 tsp chipotle powder or cayenne pepper (optional)

1-2 tbsp Grillstock House Rub (see p.202)

The rest

200g Cotija cheese or feta cheese, crumbled

2 limes, quartered

1 red chilli, finely chopped

METHOD

① Set up your BBQ to cook directly (see p.18) at a medium heat, around 160°C.

② Place the corn on the grill with the husk-handles hanging off the side so they don't burn. Cook for about 8-10 minutes, turning the cobs every few minutes until they start to brown a little.

③ Take the corn off the grill, smear the cobs with butter or mayo.

④ Put the corn back on the grill for another 5 minutes, turning often, until blackened in places.

⑤ If you are looking for some heat, mix the chipotle or cayenne into the rub. Remove the cobs from the grill, sprinkle with the rub mixture and let your guests help themselves to cheese, a squeeze of lime, chilli or any other toppings they like. (Come up with some toppings of your own and lay them out on the table for guests to add as they wish.)

BOURBON 'N' COKE BBQ BEANS

Our top way to cook these beans is in an ovenproof dish in a smoker, placed directly under a rack of ribs. That way, the beans catch all those lovely smoky, porky, sweet, fatty juices as they drip down through the grate. However, they still taste great when smoked low 'n' slow on a regular BBQ.

Technically, this is a fixin' – that is, to be enjoyed on the side – but a big bowlful makes for a pretty solid meal in itself. You could spice it up by adding chipotle flakes or chilli powder, if you like.

FEEDS 6–8

INGREDIENTS

6 thick smoked bacon rashers, cut into lardons

2 onions, roughly chopped

1 red pepper, deseeded and roughly chopped

3 x 400g cans haricot beans, drained

100g raisins

120ml Backyard BBQ Sauce (see p.194)

4 tbsp treacle

75ml bourbon

125ml Coke

100ml chicken stock or water

2 tsp Grillstock House Rub (see p.202)

METHOD

① Set up your BBQ for smoking (see p.19), around 110°C.

② Put the bacon in a large, dry frying pan over a medium heat and cook for 5-10 minutes, turning occasionally, until the fat renders out and the bacon turns golden and crispy. Remove the bacon, leaving the fat in the pan.

③ Add the onions and pepper to the pan and cook in the bacon fat for 8 minutes, stirring occasionally until softened. Sling everything else in, give it a good stir, then tip into a heavy-based ovenproof dish.

④ Put the dish on the BBQ and smoke for 2-3 hours, stirring once or twice, until the sauce has reduced and thickened. Add a splash of water if too thick, or cook for longer if the liquid needs to reduce.

Alternatively, place in a smoker at 110°C-120°C underneath a rack of ribs or other meat. Cook for 2-3 hours, stirring once or twice.

For extra meatiness, add any leftover BBQ meat at the start of the recipe – pulled pork, brisket and chicken all work well.

HOUSE SLAW

Fresh and crunchy, slaw is an authentic side dish for all smoked meats. You can chop the veg for this slaw by hand, but it's easier to use a food processor or even a mandolin. For a chilli hit, add a sliced jalapeño or two.

FEEDS 6

INGREDIENTS

½ red or green pepper, deseeded and thinly sliced

½ white cabbage, shredded

1 large carrot, grated

½ small white onion, thinly sliced

For the dressing

1 tbsp white wine vinegar or cider vinegar

125g mayonnaise

1 tbsp caster sugar

½ tsp Beef Rub (see p.203)

½ tsp celery seeds

METHOD

① Mix together all the ingredients for the dressing in a bowl.

② Put the red or green pepper, cabbage, carrot and onion in a serving bowl. Add the dressing and turn until everything is mixed together. Serve the slaw at room temperature.

RED (NOT PINK) SLAW

Ben has banged on for years about putting a pink slaw on the plates in the Smokehouses. He likes pink stuff. We've not let him, but thought we'd put one in the book just to shut him up for a while.

Actually, it looks and tastes amazing... and it does brighten the place up a bit.

FEEDS 6

INGREDIENTS

½ red cabbage, shredded

½ red pepper, deseeded and thinly sliced

½ orange pepper, deseeded and thinly sliced

For the dressing

1 tbsp white wine vinegar or cider vinegar

125g mayonnaise

a pinch of sea salt, preferably Maldon

METHOD

① Mix together all the ingredients for the dressing in a bowl.

② Put the veg in a serving bowl and stir in enough of the dressing to lightly coat. (Too much dressing and it will end up pink.) Serve the slaw at room temperature.

FANCY MANGO, LIME & CHILLI SALSA

BBQ is not without its weather hazards. Whatever the weather, this funky-fresh salad puts Caribbean sunshine in a bowl.

FEEDS 8

INGREDIENTS

2 ripe mangoes, peeled, stone removed, and thinly sliced

1 pineapple, skin removed, cored, and cut into bite-sized chunks

½ cucumber, cut into bite-sized chunks

1 red chilli, deseeded and thinly sliced

For the dressing

juice of 2 limes, around 4 tbsp

4 tbsp sunflower oil

2 tbsp poppy seeds

2 tbsp caster sugar

METHOD

① Mix together all the ingredients for the dressing in a bowl.

② Put the mangoes, pineapple, cucumber and chilli in a serving bowl. Pour the dressing over and turn gently until everything is mixed together.

PUT ON YOUR SUNGLASSES, TURN UP THE REGGAE AND MIX UP A BAHAMA MAMA.

FENNEL, APPLE & LIME SLAW

Fennel instead of cabbage and a splash of lime for a zingy, citrussy lift. Zesty.

FEEDS 6

INGREDIENTS

1 fennel bulb, thinly sliced

½ onion, thinly sliced

1 celery stick, thinly sliced

1 apple, cored and thinly sliced

1 carrot, grated

fennel tops, for sprinkling

For the dressing

4 tbsp white wine vinegar or rice vinegar

5 tbsp rapeseed or sunflower oil

2 tbsp celery seeds

2 tbsp caster sugar

juice of ½ lime

a pinch each of sea salt and freshly ground black pepper

METHOD

① Mix together all the ingredients for the dressing in a bowl.

② Put the fennel bulb, onion, celery, apple and carrot in a serving bowl. Add the dressing and turn to mix thoroughly. Serve at room temperature, with a sprinkling of fennel tops.

PADRÓN PEPPERS

This is a great dish to serve up when you first fire up the BBQ to give your guests something to nibble on as they crack open the beers. Plus, there are three awesome things about Padrón peppers:

1. They take no time to prep and cook

2. They taste rad

3. Around 10-to-15 percent of them are crazy hot, so you can play Chilli Russian Roulette with your friends

You'd usually find Padrón peppers on the menu in a tapas restaurant in northern Spain where they are blistered in a screaming-hot pan in a little oil for a minute or two. Cooking them on your BBQ is much better because fire is involved.

FEEDS 6 AS A LITTLE NIBBLE

INGREDIENTS

300g Padrón peppers

a drizzle of oil

sea salt, preferably Maldon

METHOD

1 Toss the peppers in a big bowl with enough oil to lightly coat them.

2 Throw the peppers directly onto a hot grill. Using long BBQ tongs, turn the peppers frequently until the skins start to blister and blacken in places.

3 Remove from the BBQ and liberally sprinkle with sea salt – nice and salty.

MAKE SURE THE BARS OF YOUR GRILL ARE NOT SO WIDE THAT THE PEPPERS FALL THROUGH.

COLLARD GREENS

You don't really come across collard greens cooked this way so much here in sunny England, but these slow-braised leaves are a Southern States staple side.

Like you, we had no idea why they are called collard greens, but a bit of research suggests the name 'collard' is a corrupted version of the word 'colewort', which in turn is a wild cabbage plant. Well there you go. Bet you never thought you'd be gleaning brassica knowledge by reading this book, huh?

Don't worry – to make up for the potentially unwanted veggie fact, we're going to add bacon to our greens. Everything in balance.

Collard greens refers to pretty much any kind of leafy green – turnip tops, spring greens, kale, cabbage, chard... you get the idea.

FEEDS 4-6

INGREDIENTS

2kg leafy greens, such as kale, cabbage, turnip tops, spring greens or chard, tough stalks removed, leaves rinsed and roughly chopped

a splash of olive oil

500g streaky smoked bacon rashers, chopped

1 onion, diced

2 garlic cloves, minced

500ml chicken stock

1 tsp sugar

1 tsp freshly ground black pepper

a splash of Jalapeño Vinegar (see p.200)

METHOD

① Place the greens in a large saucepan, cover with water and bring to the boil. Turn the heat down and simmer for around 5 minutes or until the leaves have wilted, then drain and set aside.

② Wipe the pan, add a splash of oil and fry off the bacon, onion and garlic for a few minutes.

③ Return the greens to the pan with the stock and bring to the boil. Turn down the heat, cover with a lid and simmer over a low heat for 45-60 minutes until the greens are very tender. Drain off any remaining liquid.

④ Mix the sugar and pepper into the greens.

⑤ To take this from being 'Mmm, they're pretty damn good' right up to 'Man, they're epic!' liberally splash the greens with jalapeño vinegar before serving.

★ ★ ★ ★ ★ ★ ★ ★

SAUCES & RUBS

BACKYARD BBQ SAUCE

Your house BBQ sauce should be all things to all men: a crowd pleaser, sweet, with a bit of heat, and beautifully balanced. It should match up to all food, from scrambled eggs in the morning to a huge pile of pit-smoked ribs last thing at night. And everything in between.

MAKES ABOUT 1 LITRE

INGREDIENTS

a splash of vegetable oil

1 onion, very finely diced

3 garlic cloves, minced

3 tbsp Grillstock House Rub (see p.202)

500ml ketchup

100ml French's yellow mustard

75ml cider vinegar

75ml Worcestershire sauce

75ml honey

180g light soft brown sugar

METHOD

① Heat the oil in a saucepan over a medium-low heat. Add the onion and garlic and gently fry for 5 minutes, stirring regularly, until softened.

② Add the rub and cook for a further 2 minutes, stirring.

③ Add the rest of the ingredients and bring up to the boil, then turn down the heat and simmer for 15 minutes until thickened, adding a splash of water if too thick. Give it a taste and add more of the rub, if needed. Cool and transfer to a sterilized jar or bottle (see p.178) and keep for up to a fortnight in the fridge.

HOT BBQ SAUCE

This is for you if you're looking for a BBQ sauce with more of a sting in its tail and a kick of heat.

We played around with creating our own Hot BBQ sauce for months before realizing we were trying to reinvent the wheel. Then, a red chilli-pepper-shaped light bulb appeared above our heads. We grabbed the nearest bottle of Frank's RedHot sauce and mixed it 50:50 with our regular Backyard BBQ sauce. BOOM! There you go. Easy peasy. Although

the result's not really what you'd call a fiery chilli-pepper hot, it leaves a strong lingering heat and the amped-up vinegar really cuts through fatty meat. Epic on hot wings, too.

To make your own, mix up your basic BBQ sauce as above, then start tinkering with some of the crazy hot sauces now on the market until you get the right kind of heat for your meat. If you need some pointers, our friends at the Clifton Chilli Club will be glad to help.

CHIMICHURRI

Call it chimichurri, salsa verde, green sauce or whatever, this punchy, zesty, garlicky, herby, salty meat accompaniment originated in Argentina and it just rocks-it with grilled beef.

You can loosen up the sauce a bit to use as a baste while you cook, or just spoon it directly onto steaks that are still smokin' hot from the grill.

MAKES ABOUT 1 SMALL JAR

INGREDIENTS

4-5 anchovies in oil from a jar, drained

1 small handful of capers, drained

1 garlic clove, peeled

2 tbsp white wine vinegar

1 tbsp Dijon mustard

juice of 1 lemon

1 big bunch of parsley, leaves roughly chopped

1 big bunch of basil, leaves roughly chopped

100ml olive oil

freshly ground black pepper

METHOD

① Whizz everything together in a food blender until smooth. Or you can make a coarser chimichurri by just roughly chopping everything before mixing together in a bowl or jar.

② Taste, and add more olive oil and/or lemon juice, if needed.

③ Season the chimichurri with pepper and serve straightaway.

KETCHUP

When we opened our first Smokehouse, we took the brave and bold decision not to offer ketchup on the tables. We figured that if the good folk of Bristol wanted a condiment to accompany their meat, then we've got gallons of our BBQ sauce to keep them happy, right? WRONG! We soon realized that no matter how good your BBQ sauce is, people still want ketchup. It's a life-truth.

We also learned that when people want ketchup, they want something that tastes quite like the classic Heinz. Nothing too fancy. Don't mess with a man's ketchup.

This is our house version that for the most part tastes like the shop-bought stuff, but a bit fresher. We also hit it with some of our house rub, which elevates it from being 'just ketchup' to something a whole lot more complex, with a hint of spice and smoke, too.

MAKES ABOUT 500ML

INGREDIENTS

250g tinned tomatoes or passata

2 tbsp tomato purée

100g light soft brown sugar

125ml cider vinegar

1½ tsp Grillstock House Rub (see p.202)

a pinch each of freshly grated nutmeg, ground cloves and ground coriander

METHOD

① Put all the ingredients for the ketchup plus 60ml water in a saucepan over a medium heat, stir and bring to the boil. Turn the heat right down and simmer for 30 minutes, stirring often. Remove from the heat and cover until cool. Transfer to a sterilized jar, bottle or similar (see p.178) and keep for up to a fortnight in the fridge.

For extra smoky heat, blend in a few chipotle chillies out of a jar. You can use our recipe as a base, then tweak it as you see fit.

NORTH CAROLINA SAUCE

The deeper you dig into the wonderful BBQ world, the more confusing it becomes. Texas-style BBQ is different from Kansas City-style or Memphis-style. The Californians do things differently from those in Kentucky. Regions far apart have their own preferences for meat cuts and rubs, cooking styles and smoking woods, and for the sauces that accompany the results. When you arrive in the Carolinas, North and South might be adjacent, but they're thousands of miles apart in the sauces they like. This is a classic North Carolina sauce: quite thin, and ketchup-based with a vinegar hit.

MAKES ABOUT 1 LITRE

INGREDIENTS

500ml cider vinegar

250ml ketchup

250ml Frank's RedHot sauce

100g light soft brown sugar

2 tbsp Grillstock House Rub (see p.202)

METHOD

① Put everything in a saucepan and bring to the boil, then turn the heat down and simmer, stirring often, until the sugar has dissolved. Leave to cool.

② Transfer to a sterilized jar or bottle (see p.178) and keep for up to a fortnight in the fridge.

SOUTH CAROLINA SAUCE

We're south of the border now, where cooking and flavours have been influenced by the early German settlers. This sauce is a bright yellow, mustard-based number – Carolina GOLD, my friends.

Plus, it's especially easy to make as it requires no cooking.

MAKES ABOUT 450ML

INGREDIENTS

250ml French's yellow mustard

175ml honey

60ml cider vinegar

2 tbsp ketchup

1 tbsp light soft brown sugar

2 tsp Worcestershire sauce

1 tsp Frank's RedHot sauce

1½ tsp Grillstock House Rub (see p.202)

METHOD

① Mix together the ingredients in a bowl and serve. It will keep for up to 3 days in the fridge.

YODA IS THE ONLY DJ WE KNOW WHO CUTS IT UP ON STAGE WITH A PILE OF RIBS AND SMOKED CHICKEN NEXT TO HIS DECKS. HERE HE IS ILLUMINATING THE BRISTOL CROWDS.

DJ YODA'S

MANGO HABANERO BBQ SAUCE

MAKES ABOUT 750ML

INGREDIENTS

1 tbsp vegetable oil

1 small onion, grated

2 garlic cloves, crushed

1 tsp grated ginger

2 mangoes, peeled, stone removed and roughly chopped

250ml mango juice

250ml tomato sauce

60g dark soft brown sugar

115g honey

80ml cider vinegar

2 tbsp molasses

2 tbsp lime juice

1 tbsp Worcestershire sauce

1 tbsp yellow mustard

2 tsp finely chopped habanero chillies, seeded (about 2 chillies)

2 tsp sea salt

1 tsp freshly ground black pepper

METHOD

① Heat the oil in a saucepan over a medium heat until shimmering. Add the onion and cook until softened, about 5 minutes. Add the garlic and ginger and cook until fragrant, about 30 seconds.

② Stir in the remaining BBQ sauce ingredients.

③ Bring to the boil, then reduce the heat to low and simmer until the mangoes have completely softened and the sauce has slightly thickened, about 30 minutes, stirring occasionally.

④ Purée the sauce with an immersion blender, or in the jug of a regular blender, until smooth. Let cool to room temperature, transfer to a sterilized jar (see p.178) and store in the fridge for up to 1 month.

@DJYodaUK

www.djyoda.co.uk

JALAPEÑO VINEGAR

We spotted this table sauce at Mabel's Smokehouse in Brooklyn, NY, where locals poured it all over their collard greens and pulled pork. Outstanding. It's a simple recipe, but pumps a whack of vinegary heat into anything that needs a bit of a wake-up call. A drizzle goes a long way.

MAKES ABOUT 250ML

INGREDIENTS

250g jalapeño chilli peppers (go hotter, if you want), sliced lengthways

250ml white wine vinegar or cider vinegar

1 tsp sea salt, preferably Maldon

METHOD

① Stuff the jalapeños tightly into a sterilized jar or bottle (see p.178).

② Put the vinegar and salt into a small saucepan and bring to the boil, stirring until the salt has dissolved. Using a funnel, pour the hot vinegar into the jar to cover the jalapeños.

③ Seal with a tight-fitting lid and leave to cool. Put the vinegar in the fridge and keep for 1 week to steep before using. It will keep for up to 1 month.

COMEBACK SAUCE

This is not a sauce you'd traditionally serve with BBQ food, but pretty much everything tastes better for having been dunked in it. Use it as a dip for wings and fries, as a dressing for salads, or as a burger or sandwich condiment. Basically, dunk it, squirt it or spoon it on absolutely anything!

MAKES ABOUT 600ML

INGREDIENTS

450g mayonnaise

4 tbsp ketchup

3 tbsp Frank's RedHot sauce

4 tsp olive oil

1 tbsp smoked paprika

4 tsp Worcestershire sauce

2 tbsp lemon juice

1½ tsp English mustard powder

1 tsp Grillstock House Rub (see p.202)

1 tsp freshly ground black pepper

METHOD

① Put all the ingredients in a blender and blitz until smooth.

② Spoon the sauce into a bowl and serve. It will keep for up to 3 days in the fridge.

HOW TO CREATE A BBQ RUB

Every pitmaster has his or her own rub recipe. It's their own flavour stamp, their own view on what base seasoning their meat should have. Here are the basic bits of know-how you need to be able to create your own, unique BBQ rub.

A BBQ rub not only flavours and seasons the meat, and brings all the flavours of the meat and BBQ together, it also acts like a dry brine, locking in flavour and moisture, keeping your meat tender and succulent over the long hours in the smoke.

You can buy great rubs straight off the shelf in the supermarket, but it's easy and fun to make your own. Most begin with a base of sea salt, sugar and usually paprika, to which you can add other herbs, spices and seasonings – dried chilli, and garlic or onion powder are a good place to start.

For large cuts of meat, such as brisket or hunks of pork shoulder, grab a small cup or tumbler and aim for roughly 1 part salt, 1 part sugar, and 1 part whatever you fancy mixed in together. (The bit you fancy can be as complex or as simple as you like.) For smaller cuts, such as chicken and ribs, reduce the salt to around ½ part.

If you're heading for a competition, remember to amp up those flavours. We want rocket power. On the competition circuit a judge will have just one mouthful of each turn-in that's put on the table. It's the one chance the competition cooks have to impress and they will often ramp up the sugar and the heat in their rub to try to get the judges' attention. They have to do something to stand out above the other 20 pulled-pork entries the judge will be sampling in that session.

Give your rub a good name, too – that's important. 'Simon's BBQ Rub' is boring and probably tastes dull. We all know that 'Dave's Amazing Rocket-powered Pork Powder' is going to taste much better.

A GOOD RUB IN A NUTSHELL

- 1 PART SALT (OR ½ PART FOR SMALL CUTS)
- 1 PART SUGAR
- 1 PART WHAT YOU FANCY

GRILLSTOCK HOUSE RUB

We use this basic rub for all backyard cooking at home. Use it as a starting point, though: add more heat, or some smoked ingredients, dried herbs or exotic spices (see p.201 for the ratio rules). If you're heading for a competition, amp up those flavours.

MAKES ABOUT 250G

INGREDIENTS

2 tbsp sea salt, preferably Maldon

4 tbsp paprika

1 tbsp garlic powder

1 tbsp onion powder

2 tbsp white sugar

2 tbsp light soft brown sugar

2 tbsp chilli powder

1 tbsp cayenne pepper or chipotle powder

1 tsp English mustard powder

2 tbsp freshly ground black pepper

METHOD

① Mix together all the ingredients in a bowl.

② Transfer the rub to an airtight container — it will keep for up to 1 month.

GRILL RUB

Most BBQ rubs are designed for indirect cooking. They have a high sugar content, which is great as it gives a lovely caramelized, sweet hit to the outside of the meat.

However, if you want a rub for meat you're grilling over direct heat, you need something slightly different, as sugar burns and turns bitter very quickly. (For the same reason, you should never use BBQ sauce as a marinade for your meat before you grill it.)

Here's a rub you can use safely on all meats headed for some hot-and-fast action on the bars.

MAKES ABOUT 250G

INGREDIENTS

4 tbsp sea salt, preferably Maldon

4 tbsp paprika

2 tbsp garlic salt

2 tbsp celery salt

2 tbsp ground coriander

2 tbsp ground cumin

1 tbsp chilli flakes

2 tsp freshly ground black pepper

METHOD

① Mix together all the ingredients in a bowl.

② Transfer the rub to an airtight container — it will keep for up to 1 month.

CHICKEN RUB

Chicken to a pitmaster is like a blank canvas to an artist. It's ready and waiting for whatever you want to throw at it. Chicken loves anything.

Our house rub (opposite) is cracking on chicken, but here's a slightly simpler rub that offers a more intense flavour.

In fact, we'd call this more of a competition-style rub than a regular backyard rub. It's more to the point, shouts a little louder. That umami flavour coming from the celery salt gives it a real backbone, and the higher proportion of chipotle packs more heat than our usual rub.

MAKES ABOUT 275G

INGREDIENTS

4 tbsp sea salt, preferably Maldon

4 tbsp sugar

4 tbsp paprika

2 tbsp garlic salt

2 tbsp celery salt

4 tsp chipotle powder

2 tsp freshly ground black pepper

METHOD

1. Mix together all the ingredients in a bowl.

2. Transfer the rub to an airtight container – it will keep for up to 1 month.

BEEF RUB

If you have a really great piece of steak, it's a shame to do anything other than sprinkle it with sea salt (Maldon's our salt of choice) and grill it over a smoking-hot wood-fired grill.

This rub works well with beef as it enhances its 'beefiness'. It's there to complement the meat, to accessorize and make the beef look good. We use it on our slow-smoked brisket and our beef ribs, but it's also great on grilled joints, such as rump hearts, picanhas, sirloins and the like. It works a treat on chicken and potatoes, too.

MAKES ABOUT 150G

INGREDIENTS

6 tbsp sea salt, preferably Maldon

1 tbsp garlic powder

1 tbsp celery salt

1½ tsp oregano

2 tbsp freshly ground black pepper

METHOD

1. Mix together all the ingredients in a bowl.

2. Transfer the rub to an airtight container – it will keep for up to 1 month.

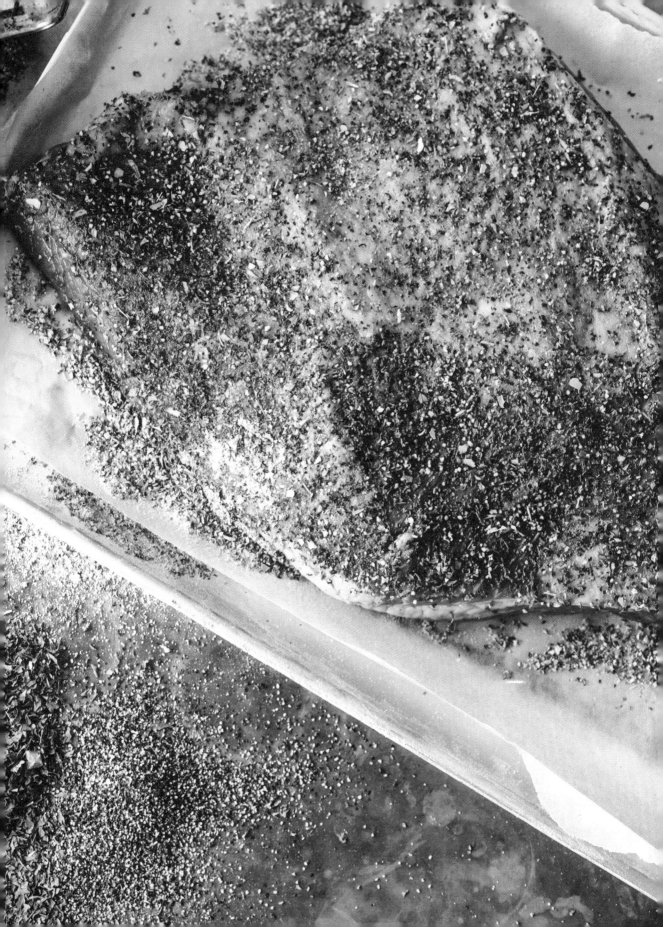

SWEET RUB

Out of all the food groups, meat is the best. FACT. But sometimes it's good to grill other things, too – sometimes for a side dish, other times for sweet afters.

We put this rub together originally to give grilled fruit such as peaches, apples and pineapples an extra whack of flavour, but we soon realized that it also works well on sweet potatoes, and butternuts. Even sprinkled on ice cream.

Weirdly, it's also tasty on baby back ribs before they're glazed – that kind of candy, salted-caramel thing going on.

MAKES ABOUT 250G

INGREDIENTS

2 tbsp sea salt, preferably Maldon

6 tbsp light soft brown sugar

2 tbsp cayenne pepper or chipotle powder

2 tbsp ground cinnamon

2 tbsp ground allspice

2 tbsp ground ginger

a pinch of ground cloves

METHOD

① Mix together all the ingredients in a bowl.

② Transfer the rub to an airtight container – it will keep for up to 1 month.

CHILLI SEASONING

It's worth mixing up a big batch of this and keeping it stored in an airtight container. You'll need about two tablespoons of chilli mix for around 500g of meat.

MAKES ABOUT 150G

INGREDIENTS

2 tbsp ground cumin

2 tbsp dried shredded chipotle chilli

1 tbsp chilli flakes

1 tbsp cocoa powder

1½ tsp light soft brown sugar

1½ tsp smoked salt

1½ tsp ground coriander

1½ tsp dried oregano

1 tsp paprika

1 tsp smoked paprika

1 tsp freshly ground black pepper

1 tsp ground cinnamon

METHOD

① Mix together all the ingredients in a bowl.

② Transfer the seasoning to an airtight container – it will keep for up to 1 month.

MOROCCAN RUB

This wet rub packs your meat with exotic, spicy North African aromas and flavours. Use it smeared over lamb or beef. Once you've fired up the coals, close your eyes and dream of Casablanca.

MAKES ABOUT 100G

INGREDIENTS

1 bunch of fresh mint leaves, chopped

2 tbsp ground coriander

1 tbsp ground cumin

1 tbsp sweet paprika

1 tsp ground ginger

1 tsp ground cinnamon

a pinch of cayenne pepper

olive oil, to make a paste

METHOD

① Mix together all the ingredients in a bowl, adding enough oil to make a paste. Use straightaway.

JERK RUB

This versatile wet rub goes really well with pork or chicken and brings sunshine to your garden. Try it with lamb, too – it's off the scale.

MAKES ABOUT 40G

INGREDIENTS

1 tsp salt

½ tsp cayenne pepper

1 tsp ground allspice

1 tsp onion powder

½ tsp freshly grated nutmeg

½ tsp ground ginger

½ tsp freshly ground black pepper

¼ tsp ground cinnamon

½ tsp dried thyme

juice of 1 lime

1 Scotch Bonnet chilli, deseeded and finely chopped (optional)

METHOD

① Mix together all the ingredients in a bowl, adding the chilli if you like extra heat.

Try a Mexican version using oregano, lime juice, chilli powder, and chipotle chillies.

★ ★ ★ ★ ★ ★ ★ ★ ★

SLURPS

★ ★ ★ ★ ★ ★ ★ ★ ★

GRILLED LEMONADE

We went to Kansas City for the 2014 American Royal and were lucky enough to be invited to the Kingsford Charcoal opening party to hang out with BBQ royalty.

Things got blurry quite quickly and we put that solely down to the delicious, tangy, smoky-sweet, bourbon-laced, grilled lemonade they were serving up by the gallon. We loved it and have upped the game a little with the addition of fresh ginger and mint. Bourbon is our spirit of choice here, but this recipe also kicks ass with rum. Or try adding a glug of triple sec.

MAKES ABOUT 2 LITRES

INGREDIENTS

For the ginger stock syrup

200g sugar

2cm piece of ginger, very thinly sliced or blitzed in a blender

For the lemonade

250g light soft brown sugar

3kg lemons, halved

honey, to taste

250ml bourbon

1 handful of mint sprigs, plus extra to serve

slices of lemon, to serve

METHOD

① First make the ginger stock syrup. Put the sugar and ginger in a saucepan with 400ml water. Bring to the boil, stirring until the sugar has dissolved. Turn the heat down to medium-low and gently simmer for 30 minutes, stirring occasionally, until syrupy. Remove from the heat and leave the syrup to cool. (It is worth making a large batch of the syrup as it will keep for several weeks stored in an airtight container in the fridge.)

② Set up your BBQ to cook directly (see p.18) at a medium heat, around 170°C.

③ To make the lemonade, pour the brown sugar into a small baking tin. Press the lemons, cut-side down, into the sugar until evenly coated.

④ Put the lemons on the BBQ, sugar-side down, for 3-4 minutes until the sugar caramelizes - do not let the sugar burn or it will become bitter. For extra flavour, add a couple of wood chunks to the coals while the lemons are grilling.

⑤ Remove the lemons from the heat, leave to cool then squeeze them through a strainer into a large bowl. Discard the skins and any pips.

⑥ Strain the ginger from the stock syrup and add 200ml of the syrup to the lemon juice and mix well. Check for sweetness at this point and add honey, if needed.

⑦ Now, add the bourbon and 1.5 litres water.

⑧ Half fill a pitcher with ice. Add the mint and top up with the grilled lemonade. Stir and serve over ice with a sprig of mint and a lemon slice.

LYNCHBURG LEMONADE®

Have these ingredients ready to go and you can push out a Lynchburg Lemonade in a matter of moments. Don't forget, though, it's made using Uncle Jack's recipe and not Grandma's, so go easy.

MAKES ENOUGH FOR 1

INGREDIENTS

40ml Jack Daniel's® Tennessee Whiskey

15ml triple sec

20ml lemon juice

lemonade, for topping up

twist of lemon zest, to serve

METHOD

① Add all the ingredients to a highball glass over ice, stir, and finish with a twist of lemon.

SOFT ICED TEA

This is a cracking drink to sip on during a long afternoon in the sunshine – one of those rare drinks that tastes like you're drinking an alcoholic cocktail when you're not. It's refreshing, not too sweet, and cuts through BBQ cuisine like a hot knife through butter. (Clearly, we prefer the 'hard' version; see box.)

MAKES ENOUGH FOR 1

INGREDIENTS

150ml cold-brewed black tea

50ml apple juice

20ml elderflower cordial

30ml lime juice (about the juice of 1 lime)

4 ice cubes

a few mint leaves, to serve

METHOD

① Put the cold tea in a cocktail shaker. (It's a good idea to make a batch of tea the night before: use cold water to avoid the tea being too tannin heavy – 6 tea bags to 2 litres water is a good ratio.)

② Add the rest of the ingredients, then shake and strain over ice into a tall glass. Finish with a few mint leaves.

To make a Hard Iced Tea, add a shot of bourbon, regular rum, or Sailor Jerry rum to the shaker.

GRILLED PEACH MOONSHINE

You won't often see fruit close to a BBQ guy, but when there's a chance of grilling something and adding booze to it, even the hardest pitmasters are tempted. We're not sure this counts as one of your five-a-day, but we can brush over that.

MAKES ABOUT 850ML

INGREDIENTS

12 peaches, stone removed, halved or quartered, depending on size

Sweet Rub (see p.206)

2 cinnamon sticks

750ml bottle of vodka, rum or bourbon

150ml Stock Sugar Syrup (see p.214)

METHOD

① Put the peaches in a tray and liberally coat them all over with sweet rub.

② Set up your BBQ to cook directly (see p.18) at a medium heat, around 180°C.

③ Place the peaches on the BBQ and cook for 6-8 minutes, turning often, until nicely caramelized and the flesh starts to go soft and drippy.

④ Stick all the peaches in a large, sterilized kilner jar, or similar (see p.178), with an airtight lid. Add another tablespoon of the sweet rub, the cinnamon sticks and pour in the vodka, rum or bourbon.

⑤ Stir, seal the jar and leave in a cool place out of direct sunlight to infuse for 1 week. Every day, you need to pick up the jar, dance with it for a minute or two, then set it back on the shelf. Choose something bluesy with a funky bassline. Make it sing and sway.

⑥ After a week, strain the peach-infused vodka into a jug and discard the peaches and cinnamon sticks. Stir in the sugar syrup.

⑦ Now your moonshine is ready and you have a weapons-grade cocktail ingredient at your disposal. Here are just a few serving ideas (each makes one serving):

• Pour 25ml peach moonshine into a tall glass with ice and top up with Soft Iced Tea (see opposite).

• Pour 40ml peach moonshine into a tumbler and top up with chilled Prosecco.

• Pour 40ml peach moonshine into a tall glass with ice, add 25ml bourbon and top up with lemonade.

TENNESSEE SMOOTH

Smooth as silk, zingy fresh and full-bodied... sours sit proudly on our Smokehouse menus for good reason. Not only do they taste good, they hit the spot with BBQ food.

MAKES ENOUGH FOR 1

INGREDIENTS

1 egg white, about 30ml

15ml lemon juice

15ml Stock Sugar Syrup (see right)

35ml bourbon

a few splashes of bitters (optional)

3-4 ice cubes

a slice of lemon or orange, or a maraschino cherry, to serve

METHOD

① Put the liquid ingredients and the ice cubes in a cocktail shaker.

② Shake it like a polaroid picture.

③ Strain into a rocks glass and finish with a slice of lemon.

Stock Sugar Syrup

To make the sugar syrup, mix together 250ml water and 250g sugar in a saucepan. Bring to the boil, stirring, then turn the heat down to medium-low and simmer until the sugar has dissolved and becomes syrupy. Leave to cool and store in a sterilized jar or bottle (see p.178) for up to 1 month.

Try swapping the bourbon for other spirits:

- use Sailor Jerry rum to make a Rockabilly
- use honey bourbon to make a Southern Belle
- use amaretto liqueur to make a Bella Bella.

HILLBILLY MARY

Mike, who runs our Bath Smokehouse, came up with this bad boy.

We've been known to throw the odd after-hours staff party in his joint and this is his way of putting the spring back in our step and the twinkle back in our eyes the following day.

MAKES ENOUGH FOR 1

INGREDIENTS

juice of ½ lime

1 tbsp Beef Rub (see p.203)

50ml Chase English Oak Smoked Vodka (or regular vodka)

a pinch of celery salt

15ml Hot BBQ Sauce (see p.194)

5ml Worcestershire sauce

200ml tomato juice or V8

ice cubes

1 celery stick and a slice of lime and jalapeño chilli pepper, to serve

METHOD

① To rim a highball glass, dampen the outside edge of the rim with a little of the lime juice. Put the beef rub in a saucer and holding the glass parallel to the table, dab the edge of the glass into the rub while turning it until coated. Shake off any excess.

② Add the rest of the ingredients, except the garnishes, to a cocktail shaker and shake well.

③ Pour into the prepared highball glass over ice and finish with a celery stick and a slice each of lime and jalapeño.

SALTED CARAMEL BOURBON SHAKE

We all loved milkshakes as kids. Now that we're all grown up and have realized 'dirty shakes' are a thing, milkshakes have become even more fun...

MAKES ENOUGH FOR 2–4 (DEPENDING ON THE SIZE OF GLASS)

INGREDIENTS

100g dulce de leche (or caramel sauce)

½ tsp sea salt, preferably Maldon, plus extra for serving (optional)

250ml milk

500g bourbon vanilla ice cream, plus extra for serving (optional)

1 shot bourbon per person

whipped cream, for serving (optional)

brown sugar, for serving (optional)

METHOD

① Gently heat the dulce de leche in a small saucepan. Add the salt and stir until it has dissolved. Leave to cool.

② Put the milk and ice cream into a blender and blitz until smooth. Or use an old-school milkshake-shaker, which is much more fun.

③ Add a good spoonful of the salted dulce de leche to each glass – if you're feeling fancy, turn the glass as you drizzle in the sauce to give it a swirly effect. Top with the milkshake then hit it with the bourbon before serving.

You can finish off the shake with a little more ice cream or a dollop of whipped cream sprinkled with brown sugar and a tiny pinch of Maldon.

INDEX

GRILLSTOCK: THE BBQ BOOK

First published in Great Britain in 2016 by Sphere

10 9 8 7 6 5 4 3 2

A CIP catalogue record for this book is available from
the British Library.

ISBN 978-0-7515-6301-6

Printed in Italy

Created by Harris + Wilson

Sphere

An imprint of

Little, Brown Book Group
Carmelite House
50 Victoria Embankment
London EC4Y 0DZ

An Hachette UK Company
www.hachette.co.uk

www.littlebrown.co.uk

Commissioned photography:
Kate Berry and James Bowden

Additional photography:
Jed Alder: © Jed Alder
Paul Box: © Paul Box
Chris Cooper: © ShotAway
Frances Taylor: © Evoke Pictures
Lia Vittone: © Lia Vittone

Managing Editor: Judy Barratt
Editor: Nicola Graimes
Design: A-Side Studio
Photoshoot direction: Manisha Patel
Cover design: Ben Merrington

Illustration: 45RPM (whatcollective@hotmail.com)

The authors and publishers should like to thank the
following individuals and teams for contributing their
recipes to the book:

Jedi Swine Tricks (© Stephen Heyes), Team Smokin'
Penguin (© Charlie Langridge), Dr. BBQ (© Ray Lampe),
Bunch of Swines (© Edward Gash), Dizzy Pig (© Chris
Capell), Huey Morgan (© Huey Morgan), DJ BBQ
(© Christian Stevenson), Hayseed Dixie (© John Wheeler),
Reverend Peyton's Big Damn Band (© Breezy Peyton),
Motley-Que Crew (© Ron Walker), Beefy Boys (© Daniel
Mayo-Evans), Tom Herbert (© Tom Herbert), DJ Yoda
(© Duncan Beiny).

Lynchburg Lemonade® (p.212):
© Brown-Forman Corporation

ACKNOWLEDGEMENTS

SPECIAL THANKS FROM JON

My beautiful wife Marie-Louise for always backing me, even when the chips were down; without your encouragement, advice and unswerving support Grillstock could never have happened. Noah & Jake for being awesome and keeping me young. Mum & Dad for everything over the years, and for giving me a lifelong love of food and sharing it with others. Bob, Beth, Brett, Owain, Daisy, Huxley and the rest of my family, in-laws and out-laws. And all my friends who have been there for me along the way. Love you all. x

SPECIAL THANKS FROM BEN

To all my family & friends for the support on this epic journey so far... – Mum & Dad this one's for you, too. Auntie Jean, Uncle Chris (RIP). Nan & Gramps, Hannah & Josh, Liz, Sam, Maria, Izzy & Woodrow. Susanna, Rudy, Geoff, Margaret, Kev, Chess & Ebon, Matt Espey, Michael Hackett, Matt Castleton, Rich Thorne. The wolf pack – Horace, Roxy, Tanner & Blade. To my neighbours for letting us use their house for the photoshoots – Gary, Claire, John, Margaret, Maddy & Nancy.

So many more people have been involved in making this book and in supporting Grillstock over the years, but extra thanks from us both go to:

Ray & Sandi (and Minnie Pearl) – for the flame pants, BBQ knowledge and believing in us.

Mike Keller for teaching us how to cook meat properly back in the day.

Sarah, our very first paid employee, plus the rest of the Festival Crew – Kelly, Mel, Lee, Karen, Rick & Paul.

Dan Chandler & Conal Dodds for making the festivals sound awesome.

Julian, Adam & Rick from Event Bars for the relentless pint pouring.

Steve Symons for getting us on the right track from day one.

Dan, Pete, Mike P, Jacques, Lauren, Hannah, Mike S and the rest of our Grillstock Smokehouse teams.

Ajith & Andre for your support.

Kellie Hasbury & the Plaster crew.

Clive Wilson for suggesting this book. Judy Barratt for being so phenomenally awesome in making it all happen.

Kate and Manisha for the beautiful photos. We never did have that lake swim.

Nicky Graimes for the attention to detail.

Ross & Bonnie @ A-Side Studio.

Adam at Little, Brown for taking a punt on us and always being as excited as we are about the book.

The BBQ Teams who have competed over the years – special mentions go to Charlie, Steve, Ed, Emma, Glen & Sarah, and The Beefy Boys.

Mike Watson, James Clay & the guys at Brooklyn Brewery.

Robbie & the Jack Daniel's gang.

Paul Summerton, our amazing butcher.

Christian Stevenson & Matt Burgess for being rad.

Fuzz & Phil for backing us in the early days.

The Chalford Sunday Service crew for relentless cocktail testing in Hoff's garden.

The rest of Chalford for rocking up at the festivals every year.

Pete Shields – we miss you!

Helen Raison for the continued support and substantial mojito drinking.

Suzanne Ducat, Ben Knowles & crew for making the festival stages awesome.

David Buxton, Tom Edwards & OASys Crew.

All our BBQ compadres – Dr. Sweetsmoke, John Hargate, Chris Pople, Helen Graves, Neil Rankin, Ian McKend, Steve West, Neil Clifton & Ryan Hill, Andy Annat, and Laura Rowe.

The Clifton Chilli Club for their relentless public pain – Jay, Dave & crew.

Guy, Reid & the Knuckle Sandwich crew – Triple D was a blast!

Pete Williams & Emma Tappenden for all the blood, sweat and tears early days.

Tim, Neil & Matt at Citizen for getting us on the telly.

Carolyn and the KCBS outreach team.

Richard Gale, and the Woven crew for making epic festival videos.

All the other photographers who contributed to the book.

Everyone who contributed a guest recipe to the book.

A special thanks to the tens of thousands of people who turn up and party with us at our festivals each year and come and eat in our restaurants.